I WAS JUST
PASSING THROUGH
. . . when the world changed

"My Mother, Rose, Age 17"

I WAS JUST PASSING THROUGH

. . . when the world changed

CASSANDRA
a.k.a. Freda Flood

Copyright © 2012 by Cassandra.

Library of Congress Control Number: 2012908086
ISBN: Hardcover   978-1-4771-0708-9
               Softcover   978-1-4771-0707-2
               Ebook   978-1-4771-0709-6

All rights reserved. No part of this book may be reproduced or transmitted in any form or by any means, electronic or mechanical, including photocopying, recording, or by any information storage and retrieval system, without permission in writing from the copyright owner.

This book was printed in the United States of America.

To order additional copies of this book, contact:
Xlibris Corporation
1-888-795-4274
www.Xlibris.com
Orders@Xlibris.com
103822

CONTENTS

FOREWORD 9

CHAPTER 1: THE BEGINNING OF MY WORLD 11

CHAPTER 2: SOMETIMES LIFE IS A MERRY-GO-ROUND 29

CHAPTER 3: THE MYSTERIOUS FINGER OF FATE 41

CHAPTER 4: "THE LUCK OF THE IRISH":

    THE HOUSE THAT JIM BUILT 49

CHAPTER 5: A MAN OF IMPORTANCE 60

CHAPTER 6: FAME "WRITTEN IN THE STARS?":

    REDEMPTION AND OTHER STRANGE THINGS 69

CHAPTER 7: FOOTLOOSE AND FANCY-FREE:

    PALACES, GOLFERS, AND MARIACHIS 79

CHAPTER 8: AN INTERESTING LIFE 89

This book is dedicated to

Jim Flood, my husband,
Leandro Blanco, producer and director . . .

without whom this book would never have been written.

FOREWORD

When I decided to write this autobiography, a strange feeling overcame me, wondering why I should reveal my innermost and carefully protected memories that had lain dormant for so many years and expose them now to the world. However, others kept encouraging me to share my saga of growing up during very difficult times in the world, as well as personal circumstances of instability in which I often felt like I was walking about in a "haze." Jokes about "blondes being dumb" might have applied at times . . . but "do blondes really have more fun?" I leave that to you, dear reader, to decide.

This "haze" finally forced me to use an "undeveloped" creativity I never knew I had that led to amazing, unexpected and unusual events, and changed the direction of my life completely. My hope is that upon reading this, no matter how difficult and unfair life is or may seem to be, such moments can serve as stepping stones that force us to become "creative" in making make a life that becomes more exciting and worthwhile. We have the gift of life and there truly is no time like the present to hope and achieve for something better, whether young or elderly. Some of my finest accomplishments took place later in life.

However, this book would never have been written without the help of others. Memories of loved ones who have passed on who taught and guided me out of a labyrinth of despair at times will forever remain in my heart as my greatest treasures. They are as live to me today in my memory as when they were here.

Heartfelt thanks go to all those special and unique people whose lives have touched mine and inspired me to develop my own unique interests and to do my very best.

Many thanks also to clever and lovely Steffanie Suslak, my "computer maven" for all assistance she has given to me over the years and with this book. The daughter of a former student of mine, "Steffie" has devoted many many hours of her life assisting me every time my computer fails or when I am totally confused by it (which is often!). Without the expert assistance she so cheerfully and willingly volunteers, always with a smile, any time of the day or night, this manuscript might have been lost somewhere in space! And last but not least, many thanks to Vikki Anderson, also a former student of mine and now a professional tarot consultant / astrologer / interfaith clergyperson / author of several books/ hostess of her own radio program/truly fine artist . . . and more (www.vikkianderson.net). It was Vikki who introduced me to Xlibris, publishers of this book whose associates assisted me with all the varied and complicated details of making this book the best it could be in every way, from its inception to publishing, editing, suggestions and much more—an amazing accomplishment in a very short span of time.

To all of the above, my heartfelt thanks.

CHAPTER 1

THE BEGINNING OF MY WORLD

I woke up suddenly—was this Tuesday or Friday? The days were flying by like snowflakes that silently fall, leaving a white shawl to shroud the decaying reminders of modern life, changing everything—just as each new day of my life seemed to be changing, imperceptibly leaving me in a continuous process of renewal. I felt I was becoming another person in the metamorphosis of my soul and hoped I was not like Franz Kafka's Gregor in *The Metamorphosis,* who supported his family and eventually turned into a roach. For answers to what was happening, I would have to begin at the beginning. Trying to figure out my life was like trying to find out where a rainbow begins.

Childhood, an innocent span of a few fleeting moments should leave one with loving and unforgettable memories to be sentimentally recalled years later. However, when I entered the world, it was the "decade of terrifying wars and dictators" that encompassed and threatened all Western civilization and democracy with a satanic medieval-type Holocaust, terminating in the systematic destruction of over 6 million European Jews and millions of others by Hitler and his Nazis. It was also the rise of other European dictators—not only Germany's Hitler, but Russia's Stalin, Italy's Mussolini, and Spain's Franco, soon joined by Emperor Hirohito of Japan, whose pilots came like thieves in the night to bomb a sleeping U.S. Navy at Pearl Harbor on the "day of infamy," December 7, 1941, which was our entry into World War II against this pact of nations bent on death and destruction of democracy.

It was also the time that the Great Depression in the USA, which had been set off by the Wall Street crash of October 24, 1929, that turned out to be the most devastating stock market crash in the history of the United States and the modern world, and began an almost-twelve-year Great Depression that did not end until American mobilization for WWII began when America entered the war on December 7, 1941.

Thus, my childhood was more like an abrasive cacophony of harsh, frightening, sad, in-your-face realities of a world gone mad . . . but thankfully, like some musical counterpoint, there were those carefree and innocent, joyful and unforgettable moments of being "just a child" that are etched into my memory. This decade would change the world and everyone in it forever . . . as it did my own young life, which seemed like a giant jigsaw puzzle that had many missing pieces which needed to be found to understand what was happening.

At the time of my birth, life was very difficult for everyone—especially between the two people I would call Mama and Daddy. Things had gone from bad to worse prior to my arrival, as these two very young romantics who had fallen in love at first sight, without taking a second look married very shortly thereafter and had a baby girl arriving nine months later—my sister named Doris. By the time I arrived, they were finding out the hard way that they were diametrically opposite in temperament, expectations, outlook, and experience in the ways of the world and were much too young to know how to fix it, if it could be done. In those days, there were no marriage counselors, no psychologists, and there was the Great Depression still affecting the country; so they were also faced with severe financial burdens. Jobs were almost impossible to find then, especially for my father who had been in the merchant marine previously and did not know what else he could do nor have much opportunity.

Into this atmosphere, I arrived with a loud sirenlike voice emanating from a tiny mouth, and suspect I was looked upon fearfully as another mouth to feed and clothe. In addition, my hair was platinum blonde, almost white; my eyes very, very light blue; with skin like white chalk. My mother thought I was an albino, which frightened her as she told me years later.

The Great Depression was still in full force when my father unceremoniously and very suddenly departed one day for parts unknown, without leaving a forwarding address, any money, or even a note saying goodbye. He simply vanished from our lives. One day he was there; the next day he was gone—as we thought, for all intents and purposes, forever.

One of the few stories about him I remember was that he worked as a labor organizer for a union, a movement that had begun because of terrible conditions for the average working person in those days. One evening, when he did not return, my mother, worried, went to search and found him at the local hospital. He had been stabbed sixteen times and left for dead by "goons" hired by employers in those days to stop the growth of unionization, which happened fairly often then. Amazingly, he recovered.

My young mother, scarcely more than a child herself, totally unequipped for life's hardships, was left suddenly totally alone with two little mouths to feed and to care for, and no way to do so. There were no "career girls" then (not in her world), nor had she been prepared to do anything in the commercial world, since she had just graduated from high school when she met my father and married him shortly thereafter, fully expecting to be taken care of by him, as it mostly was in those days for people of her background.

She was strikingly gorgeous as well as extremely intelligent and had graduated from high school very young. Original and unique, despite many serious obstacles like ill health and financial troubles, her love, care, and good nature did a lot to cheer us up despite such sad conditions. My memories of her are tinged with great love, as well as many happy days filled with humorous anecdotes. She lifted our spirits and was always fun and interesting to be with despite so many sad times she had to endure.

However, I still cannot understand how she was able to feel so loving about having to be with us! In retrospect, I do not know how she did it, but she gave us her unselfish, total, and uncompromising love. Perhaps "love does conquer all," as is said. As for myself, I always will remember her with the fondest love in my heart but with great sadness that often fills my eyes with tears at the life she had to live. Like a recurring bad dream that hangs over my head like a sword, I vividly recall those days and the sight of her tears. One can learn very young not to cry out loud which I did because one must be strong.

We lived in Brooklyn at the time, in a section only about one mile square known as Brownsville. As small as it was, many famous people came from there as well as surrounding communities, including well-known TV and radio host Larry King; beloved actor-comedian Danny Kaye; film director Ralph Bakshi; Golden Globe—nominated actor Daniel Benzali; author and former CEO of the Special Olympics Bruce Pasternack; pundit and writer Norman Podhoretz; former Rutgers University basketball standout and NBA player Phil Sellers; Rev. Al Sharpton; prizefighter Mike Tyson; etc. It also had been known in the past for criminal gangs, and in the 1930s and 1940s, it achieved notoriety as the birthplace of Murder Inc.!

On one day I will never forget, she took us to the Loew's Pitkin Theatre, an overly decorated palatial showplace for movies, as they were often built in earlier days. Plush carpeting, wide stairways, gorgeous huge glass chandeliers hung from the ceilings, while red velvet chairs with golden arms featured lion's heads on the edge of the armrests in the lobby. They not only showed movies but had live entertainment on the stage as well and became the gathering place for the neighborhood's best entertainment where people went for a "night out."

On this memorable day, my mother got onto a long line of people waiting to see the "Smallest Man in the World," also billed as an "Arabian fortune-teller." Of course, people were much more innocent in those days. We know today that "magic" can be done with mirrors to make people look much smaller, but this type of sophistication had not yet been discovered by most people.

After more than half an hour waiting in line, my mother, together with her two little "angels," finally entered a small tent decorated with Arabic symbols. It had a big round glass ball set in the center of a tiny round table with two chairs nearby. Inside the round glass ball, there appeared to be a very tiny man sitting with crossed legs, wearing white pantaloons with a red sash and a huge turban wrapped around his head, theatrically very impressive.

After exchanging a few words with her, he soon found out that my father had deserted us and that she lived with us alone. Although I do not remember much of the conversation, I do recall that at the end, he asked my mother if she would like to have dinner with him, to which my mother thanked him but replied she was sorry she could not, and we left. When we were outside, I asked her why she did not go out to a good dinner in a nice restaurant with him (probably because I was always hungry), as he obviously was taken by her beauty. She replied, "I couldn't do that because I would be very embarrassed to be seen with such a tiny man." As I said, people were innocent in those days, even mothers.

Now let me tell you a few words about her two "little angels." To my mother, we may have been perfect, but to others, our flaws were very evident. Unfortunately, I was born with two crossed eyes, each looking inward at my nose. Worse, my poor sister—much more sensitive than I—was totally humiliated and ashamed because her teeth protruded slightly when she was a child (fixed years later after she went to work). To make matters worse, our clothes were usually third—or fourth-generation vintage, very ill-fitting—always too large and permanently mismatched with various checks and stripes of all colors thrown together in some sort of hodgepodge style. My sister suffered for years because of these humiliations which caused her to become shy and withdrawn.

Another interesting story our mother told us always remained in my memory. When she was coming home from high school with her girlfriend (before she married), they saw a sign on a theatre that said "Flo Ziegfeld is hiring dancers for his next production on Broadway." Always full of fun, they laughingly and daringly went inside to apply as dancers, although neither of them had ever danced a day in their lives! One might say they were very courageous, but they were also quite beautiful—an asset for any entrée.

My mother was a strawberry blonde with short curls piled high on her head, huge irresistible and flirtatious round gray-blue eyes with long eyelashes, as well as a perfect figure. Her friend, in contrast, had very long straight black tresses and blazing, hypnotic dark eyes, also with a lovely figure; and they both made a dramatic entrance to visit the renowned Flo Ziegfeld, one of the greatest Broadway impresarios of all times from 1907 to the early 1930s, famous for his annual Ziegfeld Follies, which were musical extravaganzas featuring stunning dancers in exotic costumes. He immediately hired both of them. My mother was put on one end of the line, her friend on the other end, and the music began.

About ten minutes later, Ziegfeld stopped the music and said that there were two girls out of step who would have to take special lessons from his coach the next day! Of course, this was very exciting and great fun, but unfortunately very short-lived; they did not appear the next day because both of their parents, religious Orthodox Jews, forbade them from becoming showgirls, as "nice girls did not do that." And that was the end of what could have been a fantastic career for two adventurous beautiful young ladies who might have become famous but were born ahead of their time.

We also had happy memories of childhood, as well as sad ones. First, here are happier times. There are a few ways in which my sister and I not only enjoyed ourselves but also found a way to make a few pennies so that we could indulge our taste for ice cream or candy—as we did not get any allowance (and were even glad when we had *any* supper to eat). We became very "young entrepreneurs." My sister, who was older than I and a lot more savvy, was always the director in charge. I was her one and only follower who took orders and did what she told me to do. From this imaginative enterprise, both of us formed a very small but profitable business, which not only gave us many laughs but also allowed us to indulge ourselves with ice cream, soda—or halvah (a Turkish candy mixture of crushed sesame seeds) and "charlotte russe" (a dab of whipped cream on a tiny bit of cake in a small paper cup with a cherry on top), both of which came out only once a year in October. Here is how our little business worked—one could not say we did not work for our living!

"Feisty" Me—Age 6

"In My Best Second Hand Clothes"

My sister would give me orders for the day. One day, she told me to put one arm inside my coat and let the sleeve hang down loosely by my side and go walking on Pitkin Avenue, a main street where people would gather or stroll at night because of the many stores, theatre, and other places of local interest there at the time. I was to go over and tell them that I had only one arm and if they could please give me a penny, I could help my mother buy food. People were very kind and "pretended" to believe me. It was not long before we were licking our lips covered in ice cream.

Another time involved my natural but powerful voice for a child that was able to reach high decibels (which eventually enabled me to win a singing scholarship at the Metropolitan Opera when I was in my teens). My sister directed me to each store, some of which were slightly below ground level where one had to go down three or four steps, and told me to scream at the "top of my lungs." When I was told to go away, I was to ask for a nickel. This turned into another successful venture, enabling us to enjoy favorite goodies.

At other times, we would go over to a Yiddish theater nearby where live actors performed and at intermission when people came out for a breath of fresh air (there was no air-conditioning in those days), they drank sodas out of bottles. When they returned to their seats, we collected all the empty bottles and turned them in for three cents each, another entrepreneurial way to buy goodies. We were always honest as we were brought up to be, however, and never took a penny that we had not worked for!

Many years later when I went to Mexico and saw many four—and five-year-old little children selling "chicle" (gum) on the beaches, I felt much sadness for those sweet innocents who were surely going to face great hardship in life simply because they were born into poverty. Poor as we were, there were always others in much worse circumstances as poverty was the norm in those days for so many. Because our lives were so difficult at such a tender age we subsequently worked with various groups to help others more unfortunate than we had been.

Destiny was not very kind to Mama. Only two weeks previous to my birth, when I decided to come into this strange place called "world" her beloved mother suddenly and unexpectedly passed away at the age of fifty from peritonitis, an infection due to a sudden rupture of appendix—antibiotics had not been discovered then or she might have survived. My birth, which should have been a happy occasion was just another very sad time for my mother, as within weeks, she was totally alone without a husband, without money, without resources and with two tiny, noisy, hungry little ones who certainly did not make life easier for her.

No help was forthcoming from her family because they were having too many troubles of their own, like so many others in those days, and had also scattered to other places to live where they could find some work. Unfortunately, her father was now a widower, having lost his wife and helpmate in the small store they had, and was now alone working very many long hours each day to keep up this little place where he sold exotic fish and vegetables from all over the world and proudly was known for his extreme honesty. I remember he was handsome, with reddish blonde hair, large blue eyes, and ruddy skin. He was very immaculate and when he dressed to go somewhere, he looked like he stepped out of a store window for men's suits. Not long after my grandmother passed away, many more women were suddenly buying lots of fish and vegetables from his store on Belmont Avenue.

From 6:00 a.m. to 8:00 p.m., six days a week, he worked very hard, but never worked on Saturday, the seventh day of rest in the Bible. This day was sacred and meant only for going to the *shul* (temple) to say prayers and meet other congregants, which took a large part of the morning, and then to relax at the local Turkish baths, the "meeting place" where men all congregated for their weekly steam baths and rubdowns, as well as to get the latest news of what had been taking place in the local neighborhood or the world.

Brownsville was a place where many Jews came after leaving Russia, Germany, Austria, Poland, and other European countries—most often to escape pogroms (organized massacres of Jews) until Hitler came to power when any Jew who could flee did so, (many could not and these were sent to die in gas chambers). For centuries, Jews had been placed under strict regulations throughout most European cities, having to live in crowded narrow places known as ghettos (unless they lived in rural area in some countries). Ghettos had very narrow streets with tall, crowded buildings in which many families lived in small "apartments" on top of each other. Around the ghetto walls gates were built to confine activities of Jews and who had to be back inside those walls at a given time of day when the gates would be locked. Those who did not get in on time would go to jail. Jews were mostly never allowed to own land, become professionals,or work in many industries. However, walls did not protect Jews from being attacked. Christmas and Easter week were especially dangerous times when their non-Jewish neighbors would go on sprees and kill "the Jews," a sort of local sport common all over Europe in most countries—amazingly, with the exception of Ireland, who welcomed and honored them, treating them with respect.

The first Jewish mayor in Ireland was William Annyas of Youghal, County Cork, in 1555. In 1874, Lewis Wormser Harris was elected lord mayor of Dublin but died before he took office. In 1956, Robert Briscoe became the first Jewish lord mayor of Dublin and was reelected in 1961. His son, Ben Briscoe, also served as lord mayor of Dublin from 1988—89. Gerald Goldberg became lord mayor of Cork. **Apart** from some efforts to convert the Jews to Christianity, their small community was left in peace. Daniel O'Connell, the great Irish political leader of the first half of the nineteenth century, was able to say of the Jews: 'Ireland has claims on your ancient race, it is the only country that I know of unsullied by any one act of persecution of the Jews'. He supported with enthusiasm the efforts of the Jews to attain full civil rights within the United Kingdom. In 1846 an obsolete statute which prescribed a special dress for Jews was formally repealed by the British Parliament on the insistence of O'Connell.

Left—"Me"
Center—Mr. Todres
Right—My Sister Doris

For their part, the Jews in Ireland and internationally played a part out of proportion to their numbers in helping to relieve the general distress during the Great Famine. In the original list of the "British Association for the Relief of Famine," preserved in the National Library in Dublin, Queen Victoria heads the list with a gift of £2,000 followed by the Jewish financier Baron Lionel de Rothschild's £1,000. A Dublin newspaper, commenting in 1850 on the Baron's generosity, made the point that he and his family had contributed during the Irish famine of 1847 . . . "a sum far beyond the joint contributions of the Devonshires, and Herefords, Lansdownes, Fitzwilliams and Herberts, who annually drew so many times that amount from their Irish estates." In 1880 when a new appeal for help for Ireland was directed at America, the Irish Relief Fund and the Irish Famine Fund was liberally supported by American Jews.

Thus, Jews who left Europe and came to our neighborhood in Brooklyn were united in a bond of understanding, even though they had many differences in outlook and nationality. Belmont Avenue, where my grandfather's store was located, was a very narrow street filled with lots of tiny stores and pushcarts on narrow sidewalks, jammed with interesting foods, clothes, and other items from all over the world, similar to Turkish "bazaars." Throughout history, in many cultures, a central focus of human activity has been visiting local bazaars and one of the appeals of doing so has been that it is not only a market place but also a social gathering location for friends to meet and discuss the latest topics, whether to solve the world's problems, newest arrival to a family, a marriage of a daughter, birth of a child, etc. It was a much more interesting shopping place than most of our malls today, and in addition, was quite international in flavor, a world of its own in a larger world of others.

In order to go to work and support us, my mother had to find a place where we could stay during the day. On Hopkinson Avenue nearby was the "Hebrew Ladies Day Nursery" which seemed ideal, as she could leave us there early in the morning and pick us up when she returned from work. Very luckily, it also did not cost her anything due to her circumstances, as we were considered "charity" cases. There were very few cars then, and we would walk, she and her two little "precious jewels," to the nursery in the early mornings and then back at night to home nearby. However, it was not to be easy for my mother, as nothing ever was. This day nursery would only take children from the age of five upward, and although my sister would be allowed, I was too small, and they refused to let me in. Since there was no other place to go, my mother was once again greatly troubled. The nursery was filled to the brim with many youngsters, and they had to set limits to help those who were arriving as refugees from the Holocaust. Thus, it was decided no child under five would be allowed—and that meant "me." But as the saying goes, "The Lord works in mysterious ways," and this is what eventually happened.

The manager of the nursery, whose name was Ed Todres, a very kind gentle man who was a member of the temple board, was extremely saddened by her plight (as he told us many, many years later when we were grown after my sister had searched for and finally found him to thank him for what he had done). He said that my mother was one of the sweetest and loveliest young girls he had ever seen, and in such desperate circumstances, her story touched him so much that he called a board meeting to discuss this. When they refused to take me in again, he said in all good conscience not helping her would be morally wrong, and so, they finally agreed to let me in—the youngest child ever admitted. But, this is not the end of the story. I was brought to the nursery every day and spent many happy hours there with fond memories, one of which I will relate now as I laugh each time I recall the incident.

This was the place I learned to play with others, to sew, do crafts and puzzles, and a place where for the first time in my little life I ate real meals. Since I was about three years old, I was allowed to eat at the tables on a regular chair and sat with all the other children. Being the smallest one, I sat at the very front of a long table that had twenty children seated around it, and there were about ten of these long tables with twenty children. That was also the time I discovered something about myself, a part of my personality emerged that had not done so before. Generally speaking, I was a "happy-go-lucky slightly dizzy little girl" full of fun with many friends, who somehow managed not to get into fights or arguments like other children did. As my mother would often say, I was a very "easy-going child." That was *most* of the time but not always as you will see; I could be occasionally "feisty" on rare occasions, and this was one even as a small child.

One day, they served "tomato herring" which was one food I simply hated and could never eat when my mother prepared it at home—and even to this day can never eat it (although I eat almost anything else!). But one day, it was served at lunch where food was never wasted, and that meant *I must eat.* Try as I might, although I did not want to be disobedient and never had been; it somehow distressed me even to look at a tomato herring! I would rather go hungry and thus let it stay uneaten on the plate and did not ask for anything else.

Along came the "teacher" whose name was Mrs. Lotterhouse and admonished me to eat my food, but I told her I could not, which was the first time I had ever done that. Once again she admonished me loudly, said I had to eat it, but I would not. Very annoyed, she grabbed my shoulders and started to shake me up and back, and up and back again and again, like a rag doll, insisting in a very loud voice "eat." Suddenly, to my utter surprise, small as I was, for the first time I can remember, perhaps an innate sense of pride arose and made me very embarrassed to be shoved around in front of almost two hundred children when I had done nothing wrong—and thus discovered that even a small child like me can be "feisty" and unafraid if the occasion merited. Later in life, when I saw an injustice done to me or to others, I would instinctively and suddenly react in similar fashion and like a flame suddenly shoots high, flashes for a brief moment, then fades away just as quickly. I simply got up on my little chair, with my ten tiny fingers spread apart and slapped her (very lightly, as the little child I was) in front of the other little children who had just watched me being pushed around with my head shaking from side to side. I suppose it might have been a tiny touch of what is known as chutzpah (akin to outrageous courage).

Not a sound was heard—one could hear a pin drop. Mrs. Lotterhouse grabbed me by my shoulders, pulled me off the chair and marched me in front of her, while the children all watched silently, upstairs to Mr. Ed Todres. He apparently sort of "spanked" me a tiny bit as was the fashion in those days, which I hardly felt. Many years later when I was retired, I thankfully met him once again, because my sister Doris searched for him many years. She finally found him living in Miami, Florida, then ninety years of age. He remembered this incident in detail and smiled when he told me he had laughed so much at the time, he never forgot that incident, and that he had to "potch me in the tuchus" which I confess I probably deserved for showing disrespect to poor Ms. Lotterhouse. I suspect that taking care of two hundred hungry noisy children was not an easy task, and I did not make it easier!

Sadly, my mother's health deteriorated. A few times when she needed to be hospitalized for an operation, we had to be sent to a children's home in East New York (just outside of Brooklyn). It was a place sponsored by a Jewish philanthropist, Max Blumberg, who had an idea for a small children's "home" (and orphanage) that could provide a better setting for children until their parents could bring them back together again, if they ever did. The result was the "Pride of Judea Children's Home," located at 1000 Dumont Avenue, which opened in 1923 with less than a hundred children as its first residents. With a co-ed population (boys and girls) ranging in age from four to eighteen, it offered its young residents in eight-bed comfortable rooms the opportunity to get a good education by going to a regular neighborhood school with opportunities to develop our own interests and aptitudes. Children could stay there for as long as they had no other place to call home, through high school. There was a heavy emphasis and encouragement on learning, doing our homework every evening, and eventually, they would assist those who showed ability and wished to go onto college and a better place in life.

It was very sad for us to be separated from our mother (we cried a lot each time never knowing when she would return), and on two occasions, we had to stay there for more than six months. This was because she had to get well enough to care for us after recovering, then find a job and a suitable apartment which was also difficult as it had to be very close to the Hebrew Ladies Day Nursery so we could be some place after school until she came home from work. However, once again real life had unexpected twists and turns in store. To my surprise, The Pride of Judea turned out to be a very special place that left me with fond memories. Except for the fact that I missed my mother so much, I felt quite content to be there for reasons I will explain although oddly, my sister did not like it much. But, as my mother explained "she was a genius" and was not like other children, so she did not feel like others might. "Geniuses were different" than other people and did not act in the same way, mother explained. Poor Doris, I really felt sorry knowing that just because she was a genius she had to be unhappy! I tried to make her happy whenever I could, but she would cry a lot because she missed my mother so much.

In the "Home" for the first time in my young life, every week I had fresh-smelling, clean white sheets on my bed with soft pillows, and my own towels. We had to take care of our own bed, making it up every day in a special fashion tucking in the corners, as well as neatly hang up our clothes in our own small size lockers, which taught me a sense of discipline that I never resented, either, as I felt proud. For the first time in my life, I slept in "my own" bed when I used to sleep at the foot of my mother's bed (Doris had her own room as she could not sleep with anyone). We lived in apartments with usually only two rooms and a kitchen. Here at the Home, I had my own locker and fresh, cleanly washed clothes every week that were my own size and fitted me like all the other little girls in school for the first time ever. I felt very proud to look so clean and have such a pretty dress that was my size. Every day when we came back from school, we were given delicious jelly or peanut butter sandwiches which I can still almost "taste" when I close my eyes, as well as delicious hot food for dinner, some of which I had never eaten before. We also had choices of fun things we could do after we finished our homework—play ball, jump rope, do sports, read books, do arts and crafts, as well as take lessons in music or painting, which introduced me to many things I subsequently enjoyed later as an adult, and encouraged us all to develop our own individuality. Little did I realize how advanced they were for those times.

On weekdays, we all marched in a line to the local neighborhood school with our books strapped onto our shoulders over our backs. On Saturdays, again we all marched in a line to the local movie to see the latest children movies or episodes of series like *Superman* and even *The March of Time*, a series of short subjects that reviewed things taking place every week in the world, and thus we developed at a very early age an interest in current events and became more civic-minded. Across the street from the Home was a candy store, and we would stick our skinny little fingers out of the gate dividers with pennies in our hands (left by our mother for us to spend) and ask someone passing by if they would buy us a lollipop or an ice cream in the store, and we would give them our pennies to do so, which they always did. My favorite candies I recall, was "Coconut Lollipop" or "Tootsie Roll."

We also made friends with other children, and I will always remember a younger "child" (only two years younger than I was when she was admitted). She was a very frightened, shy, and sad little five-year-old, whose name was Edith Simon, and we made friends with her right away so she would not feel so lonely, and would stay by our side wherever we would go. One day, she "wee-weed" in her bed and was terrified. When they saw what she had done, she burst out crying, saying, "I didn't do it." Pointing to me, she said, "She did it." Of course, I felt very sorry for this tiny tyke all alone without a sister like I had, and I never could be mad at her.

On Saturdays, we all had to go to Hebrew class and heard stories from the Old Testament, learned our prayers as well as the history of the Jews and met children of refugees who managed to escape from Germany. As young as we were, we understood there were people in the world who were bad to Jews and even killed them, which had a painful and potent effect on us forever and became part of our psyche, never to be forgotten, killed just because they were Jewish. We could not understand "why" at that tender age. I was a walking question mark and always wanted to know why, but the answer could never be understood by any child, who only were very frightened hearing this and never forgot.

Here is one "surprise" that not many Americans do know, verifiably true. In the late 1930s and early 1940s, Hitler was very powerful and seemed almost invincible. Even here in America, there were many people who wanted the USA to go to war on the side of Hitler. Two American icons of great fame and fortune, Henry Ford and Charles Lindbergh, were outspoken pro-Nazis. Many years later, award-winning journalist Max Wallace who had unprecedented access to declassified FBI and military intelligence files, confirmed how the close friendship and ideological bond between these two famous "American icons" culminated in an abuse of power that helped strengthen Hitler's regime and undermined the Allied war effort.

Henry Ford, well known as founder of the Ford Motor Car Company, had ties to Nazi Germany back as far as the 1920s and subsidized the rise to power of Adolph Hitler. Ford was a rabid anti-Semite and in his newspaper, published "The Protocols of the Elders of Zion," which was subsequently discredited as a fraudulent anti-Semitic forgery text purporting to describe a Jewish plan for achieving global domination, first published in Russia in 1903, translated into multiple languages, and disseminated internationally throughout the world in the early part of the twentieth century with Henry Ford funding the printing. Five hundred thousand copies were distributed throughout the United States in the 1920s (and are now being republished and distributed in Muslim countries).

Another example was what Ford wrote on May 22, 1920: "If fans wish to know the trouble with American baseball they have it in three words—too much Jew." Another publication of Ford's anti-Jewish articles appeared in his newspaper entitled "The International Jew, the World's Foremost Problem." Ford is the only American mentioned in Hitler's book *Mein Kampf* very fondly as Hitler's "inspiration." In July 1938, prior to the outbreak of war, the German consul at Cleveland gave Ford, on his seventy-fifth birthday, the award of the Grand Cross of the German Eagle—the highest medal Nazi Germany could bestow on a foreigner.

There was also a very popular, well-known radio preacher, Father Charles Coughlin, of the Christian Front—an underground army that attacked Jews in the streets of New York and elsewhere. Coughlin's allies included the German American Bund, led by Fritz Kuhn, who stated, "I will become America's Hitler." The Nazi-sympathizing Bund had elaborate summer camps and held an infamous 1939 New York Bund rally for Hitler attended by twenty thousand people who had the same loyalties and feelings. At this time, with so many Jew haters, all Jewish people in the United States lived in fear, never knowing what the outcome would be to this horror if the Nazis would be victorious and come to our shores. We children all lived in fear of what could happen—no longer "innocent" children anymore, learning to fear evil in the world, at a very tender age.

Perhaps the only moments at the Home that were not so pleasant were weekends when we all would stand in line and had our hair examined for "nits" and then given a dose of cod-liver oil to wash down our throats! We had a lovely doctor, Dr. Demick, who was always kind to us; and she made this as pleasant as possible—we were fond of her.

She also was the first lady I ever met who was a doctor, and was very much in awe of her.

And finally, my mother was able to stay out of hospitals for a while, and we went gladly, happily back to be with her. However, I look back with great appreciation, fondness, and heartfelt thanks to those good people who gave us such excellent care and encouraged us "tiny tykes" when we were so vulnerable and needed them so much, as well for all the things we learned there that stood us in good stead throughout life. A toast in absentia to all of those kind people whom I remember so fondly who provided protection and care to make this one little life, and many others, feel happy instead of feeling so sad as we might have in those circumstances. Thank you, Mr. Max Blumberg and all the others who took care of us and made us a little bit happier. Sadly, we have all heard of other children's homes and orphan asylums where children suffered greatly.

Home at last, we lived in neighborhoods where most people were poor by any standard, and many were on welfare. Thus, youngsters were expected to go to work very early in life, and the school system accepted this idea. They issued a rule that any child who made a grade of 85 percent or above was "skipped" forward one class so that he or she could get out of school early to go to work and help families get off welfare. In those times, most young people lived with their parents until they were either married unless one was much older and "perhaps" entitled to finally have an apartment of their own, but not too many did.

"Education" was of extreme importance to us, and we wanted to please our parents. Most of us would feel disgraced if we ever came home without mostly "A's" on our report cards. If a subject was very difficult and one would get a "B" or lower, we would be ashamed. This was simply expected of us and part of our way of life, so we became a bit competitive always striving to be "best." It also meant that most of us graduated from high school before we were sixteen years of age and many by ages fourteen or fifteen. My very studious and brilliant sister, Doris, graduated with the highest marks in our high school at age fourteen. At that time, New York's City College was free to anyone whose average was over 85 percent. She would work during the daytime and go to New York City College at night, like almost everyone else from our area did, and were glad they had the chance. Many went on to fame and fortune after attending City College—Bernard Baruch, Henry Kissinger, Jonas Salk, Colin Powell, Herman Badillo, etc.

College also became part of our social life with many other activities besides classes, such as sports, dances, chess clubs, etc., which were mostly enjoyable experiences. When I got into City College, I was not always the best student because I did not like to study much, but somehow I managed to make good grades because I had a very good memory and could remember almost anything I heard or read. But to my way of thinking, I thought that was not being really smart, and I developed a bit of an inferiority complex compared to so many of the others there who were, to me, brilliant.

I had already decided to become an opera singer and actually won a scholarship to the Metropolitan Opera for one year. Sorry to say, and something I always regretted, I could not take advantage of it and had to give up all my dreams to be one, because the Welfare Department upon my graduation in those days, now expected me to support my mother. Thus, I had to find the first job I could get, as my sister was just married and not living at home, and my career as a "famous opera singer" was over before it ever began. In those days, women's choices were generally limited in most cases (except to the wealthy) to teaching, accounting, bookkeeping, secretary, librarian, nurse, dietitian, model, designer, selling, or something in the arts—most of which meant further study I could not afford.

"Fate" decided my future. If one does not believe in fate, before I tell you the rest of my story, I would like to relate an incident which took place many years later in my life as one example of "Fate" which stepped in to save my life.

As long as I can recall, ever since I was a young girl I dreamed about visiting fascinating Macchu Picchu considered as one of the most beautiful and enigmatic ancient sites in the entire world, used by the Incas as their secret ceremonial city. Over 7,500 feet above sea level lie cloud-shrouded ruins of palaces, baths, temples, storage rooms, and houses, all in a remarkable state of preservation, considered wonders of both architectural and aesthetic genius. Since it was never found by the Spaniards after they conquered the Incas, it was never plundered by them as was always the case, and is now considered to be very important as a cultural site (1438—1472,) often referred to as the Lost City of the Inca.

Suddenly and amazingly, my long desired wish to see this mysterious site was unexpectedly granted many years later. A good friend of my husband flew us there as his guests to visit his newly purchased hacienda in a small town on the Pacific Ocean, just outside of Lima, Peru. Unbeknown to him was the great importance this trip promised for me. It was a dream come true. I could hardly wait and was almost walking on air until I would arrive there.

During my many years of traveling to various places, which included going up into high mountain ranges from Norway to Mexico, I had never, not even once, become ill either from the altitude or the food of any country. But the moment I stepped off the plane onto Cuzco, the City in the Mountains in which we had to stay for the night prior to going to Macchu Picchu the next day, which was over eleven thousand feet above sea level, I felt ghastly ill. "Ghastly" is much worse than "terrible." It is even worse than "horrible." I could not even describe how awful I felt, and only someone who has been to Cuzco and had the same experience would understand what it feels like. After a tortuous ride to the hotel, I was given a hot drink, a form of local "coke" (not Coca-Cola!) that was supposed to help me. They explained that this often happens to "turistas." I moaned and groaned all night, and upon trying to rise the next morning, however, I felt worse than the previous day. It was impossible for me to do anything normal and could never even consider taking any train that day, even to "Macchu Picchu—place of my dreams" as I longed to do so often in my life and in my dreams. The next day I was not a bit better either.

Everyone said that I would definitely feel better the very next morning and to plan to go then, when very suddenly my instinct "told me" that this was a warning I should heed and not go despite all my years of longing to see this beautiful place. Now I was determined to return home to New Jersey the very next day! After so many long years, my dream had become a nightmare. Thankfully, two days later, we arrived back home safe and sound. Shortly after our arrival, the phone rang with a call from one of our dearest friends and talented producer, Leandro Blanco, who asked me how I was as he had read something in the news and was concerned! All I could think was "How did he know that I had been so sick?"

But herein lies that mysterious turn of fate that has from time to time taken place throughout my lifetime, almost as if there was "an angel on my shoulder." The reason he had called was that he had just read in the Spanish newspaper that due to very heavy rains the previous days, the train I would have taken to Machu Picchu that day was derailed and crushed by falling rocks from the mountains, and many people on the train were killed! Thus, paying close heed to my "instincts," perhaps scoffed at by more "scientific" souls, I feel very grateful there is no crime (yet) for using one's instinct. It has always served me well. So much for strange occurrences, and now on to more earthly matters.

CHAPTER 2

SOMETIMES LIFE IS A MERRY-GO-ROUND

In those days, no child ever heard of or watched Sesame Street, Pokemon, Nickleodeon, nor went to a place called Disneyworld, or had an "iPad" or "iPhone." Nor did our parents read books by Dr. Benjamin Spock on *Baby and Child Care* in which he admonished them to "treat children like individuals." Despite Dr. Spock, many of these children went on not only to become well-adjusted, successful, productive adults but also to achieve international fame and were looked upon with great respect without advice from Dr. Spock. This may have had a lot to do with innate intelligence and talent, but it did not happen without very hard work, study, discipline, and pride of accomplishment often instilled in them by parents who arrived at our shores with nothing more than clothes on their backs or whose grandparents had been slaves and sharecroppers with the dream that their children might have a better life.

Some of these people from ours and the neighboring areas in Brooklyn include Bobby Fischer, world-famous chess player; Supreme Court Justice Ruth Bader Ginsburg; civil liberties attorney Alan Dershowitz; famous TV "Judge Judy" Sheindlin; TV host Larry King; world's most famous magician "The Great (Harry) Houdini;" science fiction (and nonfiction) author Isaac Asimov, considered to be one of the most prolific writers of all times; writers Arthur Miller and Frank McCourt (whose mother took him to Ireland as a young child); Neil Diamond; Mickey Spillane; sports figures like prizefighters Mike Tyson and Floyd Patterson; basketball player Michael Jordan; sports announcer Howard Cosell; astrophysicist Carl Sagan; actors and actresses Mickey Rooney, Mary Tyler Moore, Jerry Seinfeld, Richard Dreyfuss, Marisa Tomei, Danny Kaye, Woody Allen, Rita Hayworth, Susan Hayward; comedians Eddie Murphy, Jackie Gleason, Mel Brooks, Larry David, Henny Youngman, Buddy Hackett, Chris Rock, Jimmy Durante; musicians and musical artists George Gershwin, Vince Lombardi, Aaron Copland, Barbra Streisand, Neil Sedaka, Marvin Haemlisch, Barry Manilow, Lena Horne, Vic Damone, and countless others.

Almost nobody had heard about TV (which did not become popular until after World War II was over circa 1947), or home computers which did not even enter the market until the late 1970s. Instead, children would read swashbuckling "comic strips" filled with heroes and heroines that appeared in newspapers or comic books such as Superman dressed in colorful tights and a cape was one of the first heroes, followed by Popeye who made spinach famous . . . and many more, like Wonder Woman, Mickey Mouse and Donald Duck. Children and adults waited eagerly for these newspapers, spreading the pages on the floors so everyone in the family could read them at the same time.

There were also the very popular charming and romantic, but sometimes frightening "fairy tales" that inspired motion pictures, plays, ballets and animated cartoons all over the world by Denmark's Hans Christian Andersen's "Little Mermaid," "Ugly Duckling," "Little Match Girl," and "Thumbelina," or those written by the two German Brothers Grimm who penned "Cinderella," "Sleeping Beauty," "Snow White," "Little Red Riding Hood," "Rapunzel," "Rumpelstiltskin," and "Hansel and Gretel" which featured giants, dwarfs, witches, and stepmothers in children stories unrivalled to this day and that we all loved and read. And who can forget the delightfully nonsensical tale of "Alice in Wonderland" written by Lewis Carol for his daughter but had another hidden message for adults?

All these were magical moments in our difficult lives—they were full of fantasy, transporting us on exotic journeys all over the world—giving us dreams and hopes. We wanted to believe Frank Sinatra when he sang "fairy tales can come true, they can happen to you, if you're young at heart" or when Bloody Mary in "South Pacific" told us "you gotta' have a dream, if you don't have a dream, how you gonna' have a dream come true?"

"New York New York, it's a wonderful town, the Bronx is up but the Battery's down . . ." True to the song, it was the most populous city in the United States in the 1940s and 1950s, with a population of nearly 8 million (according to the 1950 census). It exerted significant impact upon global commerce, finance, media, art, fashion, research, technology, education, and particularly in the entertainment world.

My love for music had never dimmed, and although I had to give up my scholarship with the Metropolitan Opera to work full time, I never could give up my love of singing and decided I would now prepare to sing on Broadway during what became the most wonderful era of musical comedies that were ever produced before or since, and once heard never forgotten. In the 1950s, Broadway musicals became a major part of American popular culture. Every season saw new stage musicals, and I was truly lucky to have been one of those who saw the original productions of the best American producers, composers, singers and music representing these very Americana extravaganzas—shows by Rogers and Hammerstein's "The King and I" with Gertrude Lawrence and Yul Brynner, "Music Man," "South Pacific" with Mary Martin, or the incomparable Lerner and Loew's, "My Fair Lady" with Julie Andrews and Rex Harrison, plus many more like "Fiddler on the Roof," "Finian's Rainbow," "Oklahoma," "Guys and Dolls," "Kiss me Kate"—magical, thrilling moments that will never be forgotten by anyone who has ever seen them, as well as the thrill I had each time I saw one of these, when recalling past days with special memories.

However, my biggest concern was always to find a job and make some money so I could help my mother, even when I was still a teenager in school. Because of the Rapid Advance System in schools at that time, if one received good marks, one skipped a full class ahead each term, and although I was only thirteen years old, I was now a sophomore in high school allowed to arrange my schedule in time to leave at 1:30 p.m. and thus be able to work after school.

I found a job at an indoor market, across from the High School, filled entirely with many small stalls and wares of all kinds—food, clothes, toys, hardware, school supplies, household products, etc. At one of these stalls, a man sold ladies clothes and hired me to work three hours a day. The clothes were laid out neatly on a shelf in front of the stall, and I was to work in a narrow space behind the clothes with the wall at my back, assisting customers. I was excited, and the first day after school when I arrived, my eyes lit up as they gazed upon a beige colored skirt full of fashionable "pleats." Since my salary was fifty cents an hour, I made up my mind that after giving my mother most of it, I could save $1 weekly and buy it in only one month, since the price was $4. I was very proud at the prospect of being a "salesgirl" and selling such beautiful clothing.

But, things are not always what they seem to be, as I soon learned. Two days after I was hired, I felt a hand on my upper leg and looked around to see the owner touching me. Not quite sure I understood, I told him he was accidentally leaning against me, and he apologized. A few days later, both his hands were on my legs again, but this time I knew something was amiss and told him not do that again and soon was told, my services were no longer required. I never did get a pleated skirt. After that, luckily I was able to get a job at Gristede's Grocery on Broadway and 78th Street, where I packed bags full of potatoes, onions, and carrots, which worked out much better! I spent the next few years remaining in high school working there very enjoyably.

When I graduated from School at age fifteen, I went to work at a frozen meat packing plant that existed in New York City, one of the first types of frozen food ever sold in small packages which was then coming into vogue. I still recall their jingle that musically rang out from the radio with a tune of "Quick Frozen Meats, Yum Yum." It was a family business and the daughter was in charge of public relations. She was a very pretty blonde, exquisitely dressed and manicured, with clothes I had only seen in movies or in expensive shop windows. After four months on the job, which I found quite interesting, working with advertising agencies and writing small ads for newspapers, she surprised me when she said me that she had met a man who owned a chain of drug stores in the Deep South, and they would be getting married and moving to Georgia. However, she liked the way I worked very much and was sure I could do her job successfully. Although I was very flattered, I was convinced she was making a big mistake and told her "I am not really as smart as you think I am!" She disagreed and convinced me to take the chance which also came with a raise in pay, and that "convinced" me. Her parents were nice to me, as were all the others who worked there, so hesitatingly took a chance and said yes.

The place was located at one end of Long Island City near the 59th Street Bridge to Manhattan, but I lived in the Bronx almost at the very opposite end of New York and quite a long distance from there. The only way I could get to work was to take the NYC Transit train into Manhattan (about a forty-five-minute ride) and change to another train for Long Island City (fifteen minutes when not waiting for trains) and walk about seven blocks to get there. Because of its location, anyone who did drive a car to work, when leaving at the end of the day, would always ask if someone wanted a ride to the Manhattan train station over the bridge. I was now very busy at my job, which I was enjoying and was always working quite late, sometimes until 8:00 p.m.

"I Graduated From High School—Age 15"

"My Sister Doris 18 Years Old"

One night, the son of the owners, the only person who was also working late, asked me if I wanted a ride to the station which I appreciated. I hardly knew him at all, as he was much older and seldom in the office. When we arrived at the other side of the bridge and reached the 72nd Street train station, he said he had to make a phone call on the corner of the street where there were "public phones" (no such things as cell phones then). When he returned, he told me he had just called his parents, and they asked if I would like to come up and say hello. They lived right by the train station exit I would be taking, but I told him I really had to get home to my mother who was making supper. He insisted I come up for just a few minutes and say hello to them and then leave. As I was friendly with them by now, I went up on an elevator of a very impressive building that had a doorman and huge lobby. At the twenty-third floor, we arrived, and he opened the door but locked it quickly. Nobody was there—it was dark. Suddenly, without much ado, he tried to kiss me.

Not to belabor a lot of very unpleasant details that ensued, I truthfully was frightened when he pursued me while taking off his shirt. I finally said to him in no uncertain terms that I was still a "minor" (under eighteen years of age), and I would report him to the police if he attacked me, at which time he said, "The elevator man will attest to the fact you came up here alone with me. I did not force you," but when I kicked him, he discourteously threw open the door and pushed me out, and I exited very quickly. Of course, he did not even look at me the next day at the office, but it was so unpleasant being near him, I decided to leave the job. This was not the only incident of working in places in which I, as well as many other women, were harassed in this fashion at that time. In those days, there was no recourse for actions of this sort.

Jobs were not easy to find when I graduated. In addition, there were other insidious things that were more dangerous, with a subterranean culture that I, like many, was totally unaware existed. Not too long after I graduated from High School, I answered a "Help Wanted" ad in a newspaper that sounded promising. It was for a company that sold magazines to businesses. They were hiring ladies to visit these offices to sell them magazines. In addition to a fairly decent salary, there was a small commission for each sale, which sounded quite interesting. The next morning, I arrived at the office with about fifty women of all ages, all of whom were looking for the same job as I, and half an hour later, I was hired, to my complete surprise. I must say this rather puzzled me as many of these ladies I had spoken to while waiting for my interview had been sales people, and I hadn't a clue how to sell anything—but they told me I would soon learn. When I came home and told my mother what had happened, she immediately insisted I must not under any circumstances take that job, which I could not understand and, truthfully, was a little upset. She said it did not sound right to her. Knowing my mother was very smart, although I was disappointed and worried I would not get another job soon, I decided not to take it.

The next day, I phoned to tell them I would not be there and spoke to a man (whose name I will not mention), and he asked me why I changed my mind. He was quite persistent in telling me to reconsider such a good opportunity as I would be making good money. He finally hung up when he realized I would not do so and told me to call him if I changed my mind. Imagine my shock when I opened the newspaper a few months later and, in horror, read a story on the front page about young girls, supposedly hired by a New York firm to sell magazines, were kidnapped and forced into prostitution by a group engaged in what was called "white slavery." The leader of that group was the same man who had interviewed me!

Here are some frightening statistics you may never have heard about regarding things of this kind. In the United States in the early twentieth century, Chicago's U.S. attorney announced that an international crime ring was hiring young girls ostensibly to work at good jobs, then abducting and forcing them to work in Chicago brothels! These claims and the panic they inflamed led to the passage of the "White Slave Act of 1910." It also banned interstate transport of females for immoral purposes (here in the United States). This was better known as the Mann Act. Statistics at the time proved that millions of girls worldwide were trafficked each year in this manner and had become the third largest source of profits for organized crime, behind only drugs and guns, generating billions of dollars annually. My mother was the "angel" who protected and saved me with her loving and sage advice.

Another problem I faced a few times also came as quite a surprise. I was hired to assist the owner of a company which produced TV contests. My job was "continuity director," which meant that each day, I would plan the schedule for every minute, fitting in advertisements in each show properly according to the rules of the Federal Communications Committee which regulated this carefully for offensive material to decent standards at that time. I also took care of matters pertaining to this Daily Schedule which had to be perfectly coordinated to seconds and minutes each day as an error could cause a great deal of trouble and loss of money by advertisers. It was a very responsible position, but also a lot of fun. Many prizes would be given out, and I was also in charge of allocating these and enjoyed watching the faces of those who won them. After three months, the owner called me into his office and said he was very pleased with my work and surprised me, saying he wanted to promote me to be his assistant as they were expanding quite a bit. I was delighted—not only because I enjoyed my job but also was sure a raise would be forthcoming.

He then stated he would be putting an ad in the newspapers for someone who could take over my present position, and asked if I would mind training this person, which was quite agreeable to me! I was to ask the necessary questions first about their experience, education, etc., before setting up any interview with him, to make sure the person was suitable before he interviewed her. His next words shocked me as he said, "Of course, we do not hire any Jews here, so make sure the name does not sound Jewish and ask certain questions which I can give you which will help." I was stunned, of course, and never went back to work there.

Things of this sort mentioned above constantly happened to many women but did not change until President. John F. Kennedy began to change the status of women in May 1963 followed by The **Civil Rights Act of 1964** (Pub.L. 88-352, 78 Stat. 241, enacted July 2, 1964) and signed into law by Pres. Lyndon Johnson. This was a landmark piece of legislation in the United States that outlawed major forms of discrimination against African Americans and women, including racial segregation. It ended unequal application of voter registration requirements and racial segregation in schools, at the workplace and by facilities that served the general public ("public accommodations") and in other areas of public life. It also became unlawful to harass a person because of a person's sex or to make unwelcome advances or offensive remarks of a sexual nature. I am sure a few million hardworking women, as well as persons who were considered "minorities" said a prayer of thanks when this law was passed, for now women and minorities would not have to face such indignities and prejudices as they had previously.

It was a very important act inasmuch as previously many large and well-known companies simply did not hire Jews (it had happened to me a few times), and others such as those with Italian-sounding names, without having to change their names to more Saxon-sounding ones or would not be hired! I still recall a well-known radio host in New York who said in order to work in radio, he had to change his name in order to find a job in the radio/TV industry. It's hard to imagine today, but these things were commonplace occurrences taken for granted all the time in United States history until the Civil Rights Act in 1964 was enacted! It also helped change the lives of many highly intelligent, gifted black people, who simply would not be considered for many positions because of their color.

My luck finally seemed to turn for the better, and I started working in a small office on Madison Avenue and 47th Street in Manhattan, where I worked for a man who distributed TV films all over the world. At that time, films were "videotaped" and sent internationally to TV stations in foreign countries by mail/airmail. The owner had opened various small offices in England, France, Germany, and Australia which necessitated a great deal of traveling on his part. Since I would be the only person working for him as his assistant in the New York City office in charge of all administrative duties when he was traveling which was very often, I was also responsible for sales, inquiries, various financial decisions, and other pertinent duties in addition to my normal ones. It was then I learned that to accomplish all I had to do it I would have to work almost half the night at times, if necessary, to be able to get all my work done. Of course, no additional compensation was offered nor did I know enough to ask for it! I had nobody to guide me in matters of the world and business.

However, I never realized until years later that I had been doing the work of two and often three people and was like a "one-armed paperhanger with the Hives." I somehow managed. Since then, after years of working in this fashion, I became a permanent and incurable "insomniac" to this day, never able to sleep more than two or three hours at a time. Was I just "a dumb blonde"? On reflection many years later, I realized that I had never been taught to think of "myself" when working except that a job I was being paid for must be done honestly and to the best of my ability. Added to the fact that I was supporting my mother and had to keep in mind I must hold onto a job, especially one I liked. Beyond that I knew little but paid a heavy price for that innocent error in judgment. In retrospect, I realize that it was because I had no father, uncle, or men in my life who could guide and give me any practical advice about working in the world. My sister and I had been brought up by an innocent mother who was hardly more than a child herself, who had no knowledge of the working world and too many problems of her own to solve, so her only escape from a sad life was in reading books, including fairy tales. It was truly a "dream world."

On the other hand, there was another intrinsic and valuable reward to this job as it turned out to be a very interesting position in a fascinating and fairly new industry—

Television. I met unusual people from different countries, as well as a few show business personalities who would visit our office. In addition, many countries were in their infancy regarding TV, and we would supply them with movies, sporting events, syndicated soap operas, game shows, and soap operas that that appealed to women popular in this country at the time. It was varied and interesting from day to day and, although I was overworked and underpaid, I was never bored, which was a very important factor to me. I also corresponded with our other offices in Europe and spoke to French, German, British, and South American people, and understood them even with my small knowledge of French and Spanish learned in school. It was "almost" like being a world traveler even though I had never been on a plane!

Let me describe just one unforgettable example and occasion, of a famous prizefight on June 28, 1959, when the Swedish heavyweight Ingemar Johansson stunned the world by beating champion Floyd Patterson in the third round. There was no "satellite" or other method of seeing these tapes, and as the entire world was breathlessly waiting to see them, the tapes had to be sent to many countries by the next day! I was "the chosen one" to make sure it was done—alone—with no other person to help me! I rented a room at a hotel near what is now known as Kennedy Airport (formerly Idlewild) in Long Island, over an hour's drive away from Manhattan and waited. When the slow process of making each tape was done in Manhattan, a messenger drove from that point to deliver each one separately to me as it was finished and then returned back to get another one, to be delivered when ready, to me once again. After handing the videotape to me, I had to call and find a proper airline available that had a flight going to that destination, make the reservation, and then prepare all the necessary documents and paperwork which often took over an hour. When that was done, I would get into my rented car and drive it to each airline, each time, some more than a mile away, often just in the nick of time before the plane left!. This was repeated more than 50 times, over two days and nights, where I was either in a hotel room, driving from this room and the airport watching the sun rise and fall over the airport, as well as thousands of others getting onto planes or leaving the airport, and awaiting tapes to arrive and delivering some of them just as the doors were getting ready to close for the flight! It was a hair-raising race to the finish for each videotape to get to each country in time, some of which were still quite primitive. The room was hardly ever slept in—and that is how I watched the sun rise and shine then set over New York's most famous airport for almost three days, as well as watching thousands of people come and go to and from foreign places, wondering what their destinations might be, who they were, what stories they could tell, and wishing one day I might be able to travel. I had never been on an airplane at that time.

Despite the frantic and nerve-wracking improvising, it proved to be a very successful operation and people all over the world thus watched Patterson and Johansson fight within a day or two, and three days at the most remote areas of the world that had TV—a very novel and unique thing at the time! Those were *very* long days and nights.

Although things were very interesting, it was also a time when most female workers here in the United States, including myself, were very underpaid, overworked, received no benefits, and in general, no appreciation, bonuses, or rewards. I worked at least ten or fifteen hours daily and often all weekends, as well as throughout the night, when necessary, at times coming home by subway at 1 a.m in the morning and returning to work at 7:00 a.m. the following day. Women's lib for equal pay and benefits had not even begun, and "career girl" was not yet a popular phrase.

However, "as the world turned," so did I. One time, and to my utter surprise, when the owner returned after three weeks he had been gone and unreachable, he was so amazed at the work that had been done so successfully, he rewarded me with a ticket for a trip to Havana, Cuba, the most popular playground of Americans at that time, as well as the country with the Latin bands and dance tunes I loved—rumba, tango, samba, meringue, etc. One cannot imagine how excited I was, not only to visit such a magnificent place, but for the first time in my life, to fly in a plane. I was giddy with joy; *but*, alas, my joy was very, very short-lived.

The next day, he told me he had to cancel the trip because he heard from our contact there that a revolution was about to begin in Cuba. That was the beginning of what is now known as the "Cuban Revolution of 1959" when in January Fidel Castro came to power. This was not only the end of a wonderful vacation spot for foreigners and a lovely country prior to then, but the beginning of the end for this land and its people who were now condemned to live under a "Dictatorship." When Castro first appeared, an attractive and well-educated person, he spoke very well, and promised "change" and "hope." He told them that he would provide everything . . . . and made good on his promise. He did provide change, but not in the way the people thought. He remained in power by killing and imprisoning any opposition and by turning it into his own communist state with thousands of innocent people put in prison who disagreed with him, who remained for years and years—or forever. Thus, many Cuban natives fled for their lives, and many came to the United States of America, only 90 miles away.

Most Americans were glued to their TV sets, including myself, watching in great horror at what was taking place daily even at the very beginning of the takeover. Those Cubans who could, escaped and left everything behind, including their homes, possessions, businesses, and most tragically, family members. These included the most educated, talented, and successful who had to leave with very few or none of their possessions. Sad and as tragic as it was to them, their families and their country, these escaping and often impoverished Cubans brought a great and new energy, business acumen, talent, brains, and ambition to an otherwise-laid-back city that always had been economically dependent mostly on tourism. With their arrival beginning in 1958, Miami changed to a city, which in 2010 ranked seventh in the United States in terms of finance, commerce, real estate, import and export, culture, entertainment, fashion, education, and also ranked thirty-third among global cities. In 2008, *Forbes* magazine ranked Miami "America's Cleanest City" for its year-round good air quality, vast green spaces, clean drinking water, clean streets, and citywide recycling programs. According to a 2009 study of seventy-three world cities, Miami was ranked as the richest city in the United States and the world's fifth-richest city in terms of purchasing power. Castro's loss was the United States gain.

CHAPTER 3

THE MYSTERIOUS FINGER OF FATE

The country had not fully recovered from the Great Depression until World War II ended when it slowly began to rebuild. Until then, the majority of people were living from hand to mouth, paying "bills-with-no-frills," just for basic food, clothes, and a place to sleep. In New York, many apartments still had no heat (called "cold water" railroad flats) and were kept warm in winter only by a fire with hot coals blazing in one old-fashioned stove in the kitchen, which might warm one or two rooms nearest it while on very cold days or blizzards, the others nearly froze. It was almost unheard of for a child to have a room of his or her own, and many people would walk up and down five long double-flights of stone stairs to the next landing to reach their apartments, often carrying heavy bags. Elevators and doormen were strictly only for the wealthy.

On farms, few escaped foreclosure in parts of the Midwest. Widespread erosion of soil, together with drought, turned large portions of agricultural heartlands into a "dust bowl." Banks seized so many farms that it left hundreds of thousands of farm laborers without work. Because these workers had little or no training in other occupations, many moved farther west and especially to California (which had not yet developed into the great metropolis of today), a place that seemed to promise much, particularly for farming, because of its favorable year-round climate. At the height of the Depression, though, for many it turned into a nightmare instead of a dream come true. California was hostile to poor newcomers and passed the California's Indigent Act in 1933, making it a crime for any Californian to bring indigent persons into the state. It lasted until the U.S. Supreme Court in 1941 issued a landmark decision (*Edwards v. California*), ruling that states had no right to restrict interstate migration by poor people or any other Americans.

Once the United States was involved in the World War II, California became the Pacific front against our war with Japan. Food had to be grown, people and industry became essential to the war effort as weapons, artillery, ships, and airplanes were needed quickly, many of which were made in defense factories there, and ships sent with soldiers, ammunition and food grown and sent from California to the Pacific front.

But with all its imperfections and problems, even after the war, this was the United States of America where people came from all walks of life and countries for many reasons, and whether born in America or an immigrant, one dreamed of a better life without fear and with hope for the future. Despite great hardships and insurmountable struggles for so many, the majority eventually were able to live better, their children were able to have a much better education than their parents had, and thus, they had the ability and chance to move up the ladder of success achieving goals by taking advantage of opportunities never available to their parents. In addition, when the war ended in 1945, the worst of the Depression seemed to be getting better, and so there were many more opportunities for more people to live better. Although not everyone had the same opportunities, and many injustices still had to be dealt with (many were, eventually), it is true to say that many more did live to see their dreams come true.

These dreams became the fuel that lit a "bonfire," a bonfire of hope as new technical marvels of the twentieth century helped expand the growth of the economy because of the creativity of so many who now had the knowledge of quickly expanding technology. Formerly, what was "impossible" became a reality. Everything seemed possible, and we began to stride the world like the proverbial Colossus. We lived with hope now and looked forward to the future with great expectations.

As for my expectations . . .

I recall a term from biblical days, "through the eye of the needle," an expression which came from the small gateway built in the wall of Jerusalem for the use of pedestrians. A small camel could actually work its way through this gate if it kneeled down and struggled very hard—but it would be very difficult. Who of us have not had to struggle through "our own very small gate" against insurmountable odds to get where we wished? If there is a will, we can almost always find a way no matter how difficult it seems. Here in America, it now seemed possible for most to work one's way through "an eye of a needle," if one was willing to work hard and build the proper foundation for achieving it.

At times, I felt "compelled," dedicated, and determined to find any way through the darkest maze and accomplish what I had set out to do, like the camel. There could be no turning back. But, at other times, I would simply daydream and figuratively "tear petals off a daisy," asking myself "should I or should I not do something," unable to make a choice. Thus, now is the time to tell you about three extremely important "choices" I made that completely changed the course of my life, which had been unplanned; but nothing in life is static or stays the same. These choices changed the entire course of my life totally, unexpectedly, and forever. Like bananas, they came in a bunch!

Living in New York, one may be alone, but one does not have to be lonely. There were always wonderful places to go, interesting things to do, and fascinating people to meet. My interests were very varied. While I was a dedicated "working girl" who worked very long hours, I still found time to attend college at night, take trips to museums and great Broadway musicals (which I loved and still do), study some offbeat esoteric subject such as astrology or parapsychology, or join a cosmopolitan group like the English Speaking Union where British citizens from all over the world dropped by. I also occasionally attended a social activity such as dancing or partying with a friend. Life was never dull. The world seemed to be an alluring diamond with sparkling, ever—changing facets. New York, New York, was a wonderful town even if one was not rich.

I would occasionally visit a social club which met in a small but charming hotel once a month. There was a live "combo" (band) for those who liked to dance, the ambiance always pleasant, with good conversation and interesting people. The gal who organized and ran this club was a tall, attractive, intelligent young blonde named Lydia, who was a dietitian by profession, and we became good friends (she is still tall, intelligent and attractive even years later and we are still friends). In 1961, she organized a trip to Europe and for $300, we could fly to London via KLM and return in three weeks, during which time, one could go wherever one wished and visit places only read about but longed to see (or could afford). London, tome, was the world of Charles Dickens whose novels my mother avidly read and brought home to us. They were works about old Victorian society, such as *Oliver Twist* (1839) which shocked readers with its images of poverty and crime. Who did not feel sorry for poor orphaned Oliver Twist who was "the last on the list?" Who could forget *A Tale of Two Cities* with those immortal words that began with, "It was the best of times, it was the worst of times, it was the age of wisdom, it was the age of foolishness . . ."

Dickens's novels were filled with satire and humor—autocratic aristocrats, lascivious lovers, worldly women, as well as the profound poverty that then existed, with heroes and heroines exemplifying virtues of simplicity, sincerity, and sacrifice. I was also always amused at the odd names of "pubs" (shortened version of "public houses"). These pubs were an important part of British, Welsh, Scotch, and Irish familial societies, where members of families including children would eat, drink, talk, play darts, or meet friends and enjoy very reasonably priced meals together. To this day, these pubs still dot the countryside with colorful imaginative names like Bag o' Nails, Cat and the Fiddle, Blue-eyed Maid, Hole in the Wall, Push Inn, King's Arms, Fighting Cocks, White Swan. How appealing all of this was to me and how I wished I could go, but it seemed as if fate was laughing at me . . . I now had the time, but not the money!

This was a time just following five years of working around the clock with very little pay, many burdens, no benefits, on my job with the TV owner whose offices were spread all over the world and which I had to run when he was away which was quite often, the same one I had to stay at the airport and send videotapes for 3 days and nights, and more. In a sudden distressing moment following unpleasant words from my employer about more work to be done, overwhelmed I suddenly decided to leave my job! Enough was enough, and I gave notice I would be leaving in two weeks. Although I would be getting a small amount of money from unemployment insurance beginning in a few weeks, my total bank account equaled $600! Thus, it was impossible—totally foolish for me to consider going on this venture, which would have been a "dream come true"—but one I could not possibly think of.

Now for that unexpected twist of Fate that would occasionally occur in my life. When I mentioned it to my sister (who was married but in difficult circumstances so could not help), insisted I *had* to go on this trip—I insisted I *could not* afford to go. She kept calling and insisting I *must* go, telling me since I had worked so hard for so many years, I must take time off, etc. I still insisted I *could not* even think about going. After several more bantering phone calls between us, suddenly and unexpectedly, I changed my mind. "Why" was a mystery I could not figure out—it was strictly an intuitive feeling I 'should' go, so on May 29, 1960, a few days after I left my job, I was on a plane headed for London as carefree as a bird on its wing soaring high into the sky. Freedom at last! Worry about bills later!

In everyone's life, there are rare moments it seems as if "lady luck" quietly taps us on a shoulder and decides to do something special in our darkest moments, without any planning on our part and I suddenly felt new hope and unexplained cheerfulness. My imagination transported me to "castles in Spain" with handsome matadors and flamenco music, then to the top of the Eiffel Tower in "Gay Paree" where people understood "joie de vivre," then on to ancient Rome's magnificent edifices as well as Florence, home of opera and art, after which I would arrive in Holland whose windmills and wooden shoes enchanted me, as well seeing an exhibit of the original paintings of my favorite painter, Vincent Van Gogh . . . these dreams were filled with *huge* excitement but my pocketbook was tiny. I purchased a book, Arthur Frommer's "*Europe on $5 a Day* "as my traveling companion to guide the way (this was 1960, and by 1999, it was *Europe on $100 a Day*!). I now had the sum total of $300 left to spent after airfare, and with optimism planned to go all around Europe via the European train system which cost $90 second class throughout Europe and had seats that could be opened into beds, saving me hotel fare for two nights each way, coming and going (as of now, a ten-day pass on the railroads to only five countries costs $530). Loaves of bread, lots of cheese, tomatoes and fruits from groceries would avoid any need to dine in restaurants wherever possible. Of course, in 1960, there were not many young ladies who went alone around Europe only with a travel guide as her companion, but I had total faith that this would be an exciting adventure. Not only did I eventually visit all these places and see Europe on $5 a day, but something else totally unexpected changed the entire course of my life. Again, the fickle finger of "fate" had decided my future.

"Where there is a will, there is a way," and whenever I was discouraged and felt hopeless, this thought has saved me in difficult situations because it was the "springboard" for being creative and finding new ways of thinking, instead of giving up and feeling helpless. Failure is bound to occur if one does not have "hope" of change, and I had already learned that many things in life do change. This time I had decided to leave sad memories behind and enjoy myself with expectation of good things to come.

The best part of my fascinating adventures in Europe almost "*begins at the end*" of this unexpected trip to Europe. After I had already visited all of these places and had a wonderful time, my heart and mind filled with fascinating memories of new sights and sounds and meeting different kinds of people and places that I had only read about, there were now only three days left before my trip to Europe would end. I was in Amsterdam, but inexplicably and suddenly decided I would go back to London before flying home as we could board our plane in either place, even though I did not look forward to a trip back to London on that floundering ferry where so many people lost their lunch!.

Why? My mind reverted back to the beginning with memories and thoughts of that lovely day in spring when I first arrived in London, May 29, 1961. My plane landed at Heathrow Airport and I took the underground train to Russell Square in London, recommended by Arthur Frommer in his travel book as having some nice "bed and board" places to stay that were rather inexpensive. While waiting on the station, I noticed a large sign advertising that the "Horse Races at Epsom Downs" would take place that day at 3:00 p.m. I had never been to a horse race or gambled on anything more than a $1 Irish sweepstakes ticket in my life, and definitely was not inclined toward gambling especially with my limited funds, but suddenly thought, "It *is* a vacation after all, why not do something different?" *Why* I thought I would, I had no clue except that in a burst of enthusiasm and hope, I might win some money—as it felt like my lucky day! In those days, there was basically no legal gambling in the United States (except in Reno and Las Vegas, and formerly Havana, Cuba, which had been a very popular vacation destination for Americans in the pre-Castro past).

Thanks to my Frommer's travel "bible," I checked into a charming small "bed and board" on Russell Square, near one of those very small parks which dot London even to this day, where one could sit and rest a few moments. At least the price was right—it cost approximately $2 a night, *including* a huge breakfast which consisted of oatmeal, eggs, juice, toast, and tea, and thus I would not be hungry until evening. (As of December 2011, the same modestly priced rooms on Russell Square range from $100 and up "without breakfast.") As soon as I had arrived, without unpacking, I asked the clerk how to get to Epsom Downs for the races and was sure she thought I was "another crazy American!" Since the races began at 3:00 p.m., I had about two hours to get there, and off I went once more on the Underground, arriving at the races about ten minutes before they began.

Now I faced a problem. I had no clue about how or where to bet on horses, so I had to think quickly. Looking around me, I noticed a few young men standing around a stall where drinks were being served; so naturally, I selected the handsomest one (of course, which proved I was not a dumb blonde), who graciously took my hand into his, twice the size of mine and so strong I thought he had broken my fingers when he shook it. He said he would be delighted to help me. The races were very exciting, the horses graceful and gorgeous to watch—and we quickly *lost* $20 (quite a bit of money for me)! The handsome young man who helped me lose $20 so quickly was from a tiny town named Castlebridge in County Wexford, Ireland, and his name was Jim Flood.

Fast forward to September, 1962. It was "the best of times" and the time that changed my life completely and forever, when one day in September 1962, a handsome young man stepped off a plane at Idlewild (now called Kennedy) Airport in New York, the Irishman Jim Flood that I met on my trip to London at Epsom Downs, who came to visit me, and also the day my world and life would change forever. May 29 certainly had been my "lucky day"—in 1961, and exactly two years later when we also were married on May 29, 1963 (never realizing it was the same date, May 29, that we met two years previously, until years later).

There is an old saying that important things happen in threes—and the next three years proved to be the most unusual I have ever encountered until then. It was the "Age of Aquarius," with its music shouting out "this is the dawning of the age of Aquarius" that set the stage for a worldwide revolution of social values not only to "let your hair down" and "let the sun shine in" with its message of "peace and love," and performances of "Hair" which shocked older generations as nude bodies paraded onstage. Rocking the music industry, the Beatles appeared on Ed Sullivan's TV Show as these amateurs were writing their own songs without songwriters. And, nobody will ever forget the magnetic Elvis Presley's hip-swaying, guitar playing, and singing, who since the 1950s continued to mesmerize fans all over the world with his rock 'n' roll, ballads, and gospel.

It was also the time of the great "space exploration" race with Russia, culminating in the extraordinary "Apollo" program, the first manned spacecraft landing on the moon with Neil Armstrong, the first human, ever to stand on it (confirming to all it was not made of "green cheese," but now could say there was a "man on the moon!"). Satellites, computerization, touch-tone phones, and electronics just in their infancy started to change the entire concept of communications forever. It was also the age of the first "heart transplant" by Dr. Christiaan Barnard of South Africa, as well as the "pill," the microwave, Teflon, pacemakers, and other extraordinary things and events, too incredible for most of us to imagine even a decade before, and now took place in the fabric of life changing it forever. That was the "best of times . . ." My life also changed completely

Since I returned home from my trip, Jim and I had been corresponding by mail steadily as phones were prohibitively expensive then and the Internet was not a word almost anyone had ever heard. I had gotten to know Jim quite well through his interesting letters which surprised and impressed me a great deal with the wonderful quality of his writing and content. He wrote many long letters every two weeks, about working together with his brother Michael in London in a small business of their own, about his very kindly landlady who treated them like her sons and fed them well, about his wonderful, kind, and caring mother (it eventually turned out I was so lucky as to have the perfect mother-in-law—but we were separated by three thousand miles! Life plays games.). He told me about his fifteen siblings back home in Ireland, about the fact that he had joined the Irish navy when he was fifteen (yes, Ireland's navy actually had two or three ships then), and how he had worked in Scotland building a dam, so I felt I knew a lot about him when he arrived little more than a year after we first met. From that moment on, there were only pleasant memories despite problems we faced and from the first day, we faced challenges as he soon decided to stay.

He needed a place to live as well as a job. However, the very day he was to arrive was the day my boss sent me to Chicago to do some work. I would be gone for a week leaving him alone in "big bad ole' New York City," the city that never sleeps.

While I was in Chicago he stayed at the YMCA (Young Men's Christian Association) in mid-Manhattan and had many adventures which were both interesting and bewildering. After I returned, it was time to find him a place to stay and a job; thus, we set out on an unknown journey. New York was a very expensive place in which to live, but being trained as a skilled carpenter, he would have to join the Carpenters Union in order to be able to work in New York City. Little did we know it was next to impossible to get into this union even for Americans. We put on our thinking caps and hoped for the best—but had to use imagination to accomplish finding him a place to stay and a job. We were undaunted.

CHAPTER 4

"THE LUCK OF THE IRISH": THE HOUSE THAT JIM BUILT

We now faced these two problems. New York was an expensive place to live and Jim's funds were very limited. What to do? A bell went off in my head! Why not look in the phone book under the word "Irish" to see if I could find something that might give us a hint and delighted, saw a listing which I think (now forty years later) was called the "Irish Institute." Almost magically, it was as if "a lucky leprechaun" was there to help us. We received an answer to one problem.

Nearly 8 million people were living in New York City then, a city composed of five boroughs (Manhattan, Brooklyn, the Bronx, Queens, and Staten Island). Like the proverbial needle in a haystack, they found him a place exactly three blocks from where I lived that was quite affordable. It was in the home of an Irish family who rented rooms to lads coming from "the old sod" (as the expression went), somewhat like the "bed and board" accommodations in Ireland. It was a homelike, cozy place to sleep and have breakfast as well as supper included. It did not matter that he had to share one bed with another lad, because Jim, one of sixteen children, had lived in a rather small house in Ireland and had always shared the "boy's bed" with at least two or more brothers at one time, and never had a bed of his own (the sisters did the same with each other). Besides, even in this country then, it was rare that a child ever had a room of one's own—times have changed, of course.

Since the Irish like to give people "nicknames," this new friend, who looked very much like Jimmy Cagney, the famous actor, was called "Mingy" by Jim, and they soon became very good friends. When Mingy met and married a charming very pretty Irish gal (like most are), they returned to live in Ireland and were able to open their own butcher shop from money they had saved while working here. Whenever Jim returns to Ireland every few years to visit his family, he and Mingy still find time to get together and have remained friends since 1961.

Now Jim had to find a job. This was a lot more complicated and difficult task than finding a room. It was virtually impossible for him to get into the Carpenters Union, but paradoxically, New York City was strictly a place one *had* to be a member of the Union to *get* a job (commonly called a "union town"), and jobs at that time were difficult to find. We hoped for a little help from the leprechauns to solve this one!

I, who knew *absolutely* nothing at all about the construction industry, and had never known anyone who worked in it, was totally clueless about the construction industry, or how I should help find a job for Jim . . . luckily that lasted for only a minute. I was now working at a new job (described later) and was alone in my office when, on my lunch hour, I opened up the Yellow Pages Directory that the phone company distributed which listed "Businesses" in the New York City area, and turned to those pages marked "Construction Companies."

With the phone in one hand and the other leafing through the phone book, I phoned every union (quite a few then in New York City). One by one, each told me they did not have any jobs, would not use a non-union member, and were not taking apprentices. It was very discouraging. About two hours later and feeling rather "blue" by then, I suddenly heard a voice on the other end of the line say, "We can use a man like him. Tell him to come tomorrow at 7:30 a.m.!" The only question I asked was, "What is the address?" (Probably in shock!) They did hire him—to work on an exciting and important project, building the Verrazano Bridge. The Bridge would be 2.7 miles long and have the largest span for bridges in the world at the time. Here is an excerpt from the book *The Great Bridge* (Young and Rethi):

> The "Verrazano Bridge" was named after Giovanni Verrazano who first sailed into New York Bay in 1524 . . . Under normal conditions, the 5-mile crossing to Manhattan could be made in half an hour to Manhattan (from either New Jersey or Staten Island and Brooklyn where many people who worked in Manhattan

were living) . . . *but if the bay was heavy with ice, or if a fog suddenly closed in . . . could take much longer. On clear days, when the ferries had no trouble in making their crossings on schedule, they were often so crowded, particularly on summer weekends, that drivers had to wait for hours just to get to one.* [The crossing is now made in only a few minutes!]

Thus, with this monumental project, Jim's life suddenly became much more exciting than we both had expected! In fact, *too exciting*! The first day on the job, he found himself going, going, going . . . up, up, up, higher and higher, until he reached 780 feet (about the height of the Eiffel Tower) in a rickety and very narrow cage that looked like it was made for wild animals, until not much was visible except for the white clouds, blue sky, Hudson River below, and small moving objects—cars that looked like toys, with winds howling at thirty miles an hour. He was definitely not thrilled being in that rickety cage, but when he arrived at the top, he faced his worst moment.

He very precariously stepped out onto "nothing" but a chain-link fence that was swaying up and back like a hammock during a hurricane, swinging to and fro. Since there had been no wind below, up there the wind was whistling and blowing wildly at about thirty miles an hour. For a few seconds he "froze," until he heard a voice shout "you, get over there"—and watched his partner proceed to bounce up and down on the meshlike chain links. There was now no place for him to run, and he must face the inevitable. It took a few seconds as he collected his thoughts and said to himself, "If he can do it so can I." Bouncing up and down was like walking on top of balls on a tightrope, and fearfully holding onto the catwalk hand rail only three-fourths of an inch thick, he edged his way to his assigned station as the bridge swayed wildly in the wind. They were supposed to wait at their stations until a huge wheel, which went up and back every half hour between Brooklyn and Staten Island, would come rolling by carrying two cables. These two cables would have to be put carefully in place by the two men each at opposite sides, eventually to form one very strong cable measuring three feet in diameter needed to support the entire bridge when completed.

While they waited each day for the cable to arrive, which usually took half an hour, they had a bit of idle time. Jim, not wanting to be bored, just watching flotsam and jetsam float by, originated some games they could play to pass the time. First, they would throw some pebbles into the water and the one whose pebble got there first won a small prize. Another interesting bit of fun was watching police cars that would park near the bottom of the bridge waiting for speeders to pass by on the Belt

Parkway, and taking bets on whether the speeders would be caught and if he or she got a ticket. However, the very best idea originated when he first arrived . . . it was so unique that many years later when I was watching TV's "History Channel" in which they described how the bridge was built, I heard them mention this although they did not give him any credit for originating it. Here is that story:

Since there was only half an hour for lunch time, it would be very hard for him to go up and down in that rickety "cage" to get lunch at a food truck parked nearby. Normally, Jim brought his lunch with him from home, but one day forgot it. He only had half an hour so he quickly devised a ingenious and unique way to get down to buy his lunch at the food truck and still be back in time to eat lunch. Cables hung like hammocks with the center of one cable curving down near the ground; so, he put his "hard hat" inside the cable, sat in the hat, grasped the sides of the cable very tightly, then slid down 780 feet from up in the air and . . . whooshhh! down he went, at least sixty miles an hour, holding on *very* tightly to when he reached nearly to the bottom and saw a ladder nearby, ran down the ladder steps and over to the lunch truck, brought his lunch and returned, this time going up by elevator and ate. After he did this, many of the men started doing the same thing, and this was what I heard on TV's History Channel that night. I laughed out loud as I did when I first heard about it! Interesting, also, was that the famous fighter, James Braddock worked on the Bridge the same time Jim did, but unfortunately Jim never met him. Over twelve thousand men had worked on the Verrazano Bridge by the time it was completed, and they were each given a special medallion upon completion which Jim still has.

We were both now working steadily, and a few days prior to our wedding which was set for May 29, 1963, we were on a highway in the neighboring state of New Jersey. It was Friday evening, and we had just purchased our sleek, modern shiny black bedroom set with turquoise glass insets. On our way back to New York, Jim mentioned he had an aunt who lived in Chicago whom he had never met. You may recall I had been sent to Chicago by my employer the day Jim arrived in New York in September 1962 and during that trip met and became friendly with a nice gal who invited me to visit her if I had a chance to return. Since there was no time like the present, we seized the moment!

We decided that since Chicago was "only" sixteen hours away, he could visit his aunt and stay the night, and I would visit my new friend, and still be back to work on time Monday morning. When one is young, one can go for hours on end without feeling any pain! Reaching the toll booth on the George Washington Bridge, we asked the collector how to get to Chicago, got directions (and wondered what he thought of us planning to drive nearly eight hundred miles and fifteen hours away without having knowledge of what we were doing!), went home to pick up some clothes, and an hour later were merrily on our way to Chicago. Jim visited his aunt, I visited my friend, and very early Sunday morning, at 6:00 a.m., Jim picked me up at my friend's place; and off we went, each having spent a very pleasant day in our own fashion, but this was not to be the end of this dashing weekend tale!

While driving back, Jim told me he had always wanted to see Niagara Falls, a beautiful well-known sight on the border of northern New York State and the Canadian border. Since I had never seen it either, it seemed like a delightful idea. We did not even mind that it was another four hundred miles to get from Chicago to Niagara Falls and approximately four hundred miles back to the Bronx from Niagara Falls, a total of over 880 miles. We could do it all! Youth is grand, and love is blind.

We finally arrived at Buffalo, the city we had to enter to get to Niagara Falls, and were suddenly caught in a traffic jam that lasted two hours after having driven over 450 miles without any traffic jams! We finally did get to view the Falls and walk around a bit, but did not have time to see it all and headed back to the Bronx. It was a very long drive, and the skies darkened a few hours before we were to arrive. We were so tired when we finally reached the George Washington Bridge, less than an hour from home, that Jim almost wanted to get out and kiss the floor of the George Washington Bridge! Improbable as it may sound, as soon as we arrived at my house, the car broke down! It was just a stroke of good luck it did not happen before! It was nearly 2:00 a.m. the following morning when we arrived, but Jim was at work at the bridge in time the next day, and I went to my job on Park Avenue in Manhattan, arriving before 9:00 a.m. We laugh each time we reminisce about this adventurous weekend we'll never forgot.

After his work at the bridge was done, he still could not get into the Carpenters Union. However, I do recall a very interesting job offer he received. In the early 1970s, he was once again out of work even though he had finally gotten into in the Union. This time, however, it was due to a recession in the United States and most other industrialized countries in the world, caused by oil embargoes of OPEC members (Arab petroleum countries), the major source of imported oil in the world at the time. Once more, we—like so many others—faced a challenge. Once again, my "fingers did the walking" in the Yellow Pages, and this time, I wrote a letter to each construction company. Shortly thereafter, we received one very positive and interesting answer—an offer to work on the Alaskan Pipeline. But the job offer had one major flaw.

Outlining a bit of background about oil in Alaska, oil explorers drilled Alaska's first oil well in 1896 and found modest amounts of oil, but were insufficient to justify development, or that is what as they said. However, some years later, oil was discovered in Prudhoe Bay, and they needed a way to transport crude oil from Alaska's North Slope to refineries in the States, which were then called the Lower '48 (in 1959, Alaska and Hawaii became the last two states to join the USA and are the only states not connected to the others on the mainland). After many methods were considered, they chose to build a pipeline. Tens of thousands of people went to work on the pipeline, attracted by high-paying jobs at a time when the USA was undergoing a recession, resulting in a "boomtown" atmosphere in a place called Valdez (pronounced "Val-deez"), which is now called the "Switzerland of Alaska." Valdez is a scenic seacoast town with gorgeous mountain scenery, and while it now is rated among the state's top attractions, it was not so in 1964 when it was hit by an earthquake. As an aftermath, Valdez was perched precariously on a ledge, ready to topple in a future landslide. Rather than abandon their homes, citizens literally moved the town four miles away, some by moving their homes but most by building modern contemporary structures.

When the pipeline began, although the pay was very high, workers endured long working hours, freezing cold temperatures, difficult terrain, and brutal conditions, which not only hampered construction, but also took a human toll—more than thirty-two workers were killed. Jim's decision *not* to go really was "all for the best." The reason he did not go was the clothes he would have to wear—when he took a look at them, he quickly made his decision. However, once again, a totally unexpected surprise changed our lives again.

March 18, 1969, with snow falling heavily in near-blizzard conditions, found me driving thirty-one miles from New York City to Morristown, New Jersey, having to peer all the way to see underneath a broken windshield, with a check for $15,000, going to an auction. Where had this mysterious $15,000 needed for an unusual and sudden auction come from?

My sister, with her husband and their two small boys, were living in a small town called Lincoln Park, New Jersey, on an old farmhouse built in the 1890s surrounded by two and a half acres of lovely old trees. All her life, my sister had dreamed of having her own home—she was much more domesticated than I, and longed most for the home she never had as a child, a dream come true for her. One day, as she looked out of her kitchen window while washing dishes, she saw her car being towed away! She was in shock when she soon found out that her husband who owned a small printing shop had gone bankrupt. He had not paid his bills and in addition to losing her car, she would be losing her house!

Her husband refused to ever discuss finances with her and had never told her anything about the pending bankruptcy. It is almost impossible to truly describe and feel the depth of heartbreak, anguish, and sorrow that permeates the spirit, heart, and mind forever of anyone who must face and live with a tragedy of this sort. It is even painful for me to recall this moment so many years later, knowing what my sister faced, which left her heartbroken, having to find another place to rent, move away as soon as possible to another town, and leave the home she loved behind her and suddenly finding out that they were penniless and bankrupt.

Although we were somewhat thrifty, Jim and I had very little money saved. I had finally left my latest job after working ten to fifteen hours daily for little pay under great pressure for five years, so one day, voila! I suddenly said goodbye to my employer. However, when I left, although my "boss" never believed I would go, we parted in a friendly fashion (luckily!). I have always believed it pays to part in a friendly fashion, if possible, and this time it turned out to be a lucky "break."

He owed the bank $6,000. My sister told me how hurt she was and was discouraged because although she finally managed to borrow enough money from one of her husband's relatives to pay them, the bank accepted the payment but then told her it was not enough and they owed more. They did not return the $6,000 to her and set a date for the auction. My sense of justice now became a bit outraged, and I had to find some sort way to ensure the bank did not make any more money other than what was owed. Although my sister said she would never move back into that house again, I told her I was going to find a way to buy that house at auction even though we were contented New York City cliff dwellers and had never thought of buying a house previously. Jim was rather skeptical (quite naturally!), since we hardly had any money saved at the time.

I put my little thinking cap on, and once again, that little bell went off. Aha, the only person I know who might have any money to lend for the auction would be my former employer whom I no longer worked for. There were only a few days left before the auction, and so I paid him a visit. He was more than a bit surprised when I told him the reason was I needed to borrow $15,000 and explained but he refused because he felt it was not a good deal. A bit disappointed, I left his office. On my way out, his very spirited secretary who was from Peru, with a bit of "spitfire," heard what happened, stamped her rather dainty small feet and said, "How *could* he do this to you—you worked so hard for him for so many years and helped him build up this business—no, no, no."

I then got angry too over the injustice of it. I had worked very hard for little pay and he had finally become successful so I went back to his office and repeated those words—and a miracle happened! He picked up the phone, called his bank and told them to lend me the money. He also told me the loan must be repaid within three months and that if I did not pay it back, he would take the property. Although I knew absolutely nothing about auctions, real estate, buying houses, bank loans, mortgages, and less about money, I was "whistling in the wind" when I told him cheerfully, of course, we would pay him back on time, not having the slightest idea of how or if we would or could get a mortgage (whatever that was) by then but was sure I would find a way.

With the check firmly tucked inside my handbag, I was euphoric, having never had more than a few hundred dollars at one time before. A few days later, I, the consummate cliff dweller, was heading to buy a very old house at my very first auction, in one of the worst blizzards that had occurred in years, going from New York City to Morristown, New Jersey, twenty-six miles away, squinting all the way to peek underneath a broken windshield, arriving at my destination three hours later (normally less than a one hour trip).

Because of the very bad weather, few people were able to drive and thus did not show up, with the exception of two entrepreneurs who were clients of my sister's former attorney. Although he had tried to save her house, he could not. It was a fairly important piece of property at the time for the two entrepreneurs (who were builders) because it was zoned for business and residential use, and they had intended to put up a business building. Luck was again on my side—the attorney proved to be honest and advised me that he had no idea I wanted the house prior to that day and that, when he found out, told his two clients not to bid against me unless I could not meet the requirements. After that, all I remember clearly was the auctioneer saying—going, going, gone—and in a daze, I realized I was the new owner of my sister's house!

That was just the beginning. The house, which was built of wood in the 1880s, had been deserted and boarded up in lawsuit legalities and, after having been neglected and left alone for a few years, was in very bad condition. Upon closer inspection after the auction, Jim and I realized nothing could be done to repair it properly, and it was best to tear it down, leaving only studs, roof, and basement from which Jim could rebuild almost an entirely new house. Anyone who has ever owned a house can imagine what that might cost; it was prohibitive, and we had *no* money! Again, it was time for some creative "thinking." What could we possibly do to build a new home, without any money, now owing $15,000 which had to be repaid in three months?

At the time, there was a weekly newspaper called *WANT AD PRESS*, which listed free advertisements from people who wanted to sell items of all kinds, including building materials. One of the ads stated someone was selling old windows plus two toilets, two bathroom vanities and two bathtubs for $200, which we could just about afford, although we still had not found a way to purchase the most important item—lumber to rebuild the entire house! This ad, however, was worth investigating even though the man who advertised lived in Long Island, a two-hour drive from us, so Jim went by himself on the weekend. What happened next turned into another unbelievable surprise.

The man was from Germany, and as most Germans do, had taken excellent care of his home and property, and had torn down an old house on his property to build a new home for his daughter who was getting married. All the windows, toilets, bathtubs, and vanities proved to be in excellent condition, and Jim bought them, stating he would have to come back with a truck because his car could not accommodate all the materials. It was then Jim noticed an entire load of wood piled in the back of the property and asked what he was going to do with the lumber. Although I had never met this gentleman, I will forever call him "this lovely wonderful man," because that is just what he turned out to be, and will always remember him and his kindness. He told Jim that this was the wood he had taken from the old house he pulled down and did not need anymore. Not only did he offer to give it to Jim free of charge, he also took out all the nails that were still embedded and it was all ours for the same $200! We were ecstatic! Words could not express the exultation we felt—we literally jumped for joy.

Now we had all the basics for Jim to begin building the house except money to hire help, which meant that he would have to do it all by himself—a formidable, dauntless task that only the young and the very foolish could have entertained. Thanks to Jim's extraordinary ability, stamina, and skill as a carpenter, as well as his courage and unremitting determination, he uncomplainingly stepped up to this insurmountable Herculean task ahead of him. With the help of two good friends on occasional weekends, plus a lot of sweat and tears (and a little blood when he cut himself), he worked furiously (mostly by himself) to meet the deadline so that we could pay back my former employer and get a mortgage, an almost-impossible feat, since he also had to work daily on his regular full-time job in addition!

"One Day After Jim Met Me"
On London Bridge May 30, 1961

Jim had a job as a carpenter at the time, so after work every day, he would drive to the house in Lincoln Park and work there until dark, then drive home to the Bronx roughly thirty miles but more than fifty minutes away as it was over a bridge and highways that were normally very crowded. On weekends, he would work from early morning until dark. Jim's boss agreed that he would allow him to obtain certain materials and the cost would be deducted from his pay, which meant Jim did not have any paycheck for months. Luckily, we were able to pay our bills because I was now working again for my former boss as I had agreed to come back when he loaned me the money. Luckily, he finished the project just in time to get a mortgage and now would be able to pay off our loan to the bank.

But, once again, another obstacle . . . mortgages were not readily being given for some reason I did not understand, and once again, a stroke of good luck came our way. I asked my sister's lawyer if he knew how I could find bank who would give us a mortgage, and he helped us get one. Just in time, we were able to pay off the loan to the bank, obtain the mortgage, and move into the house (the same date we met in 1961, and the same date we married May 29, 1963, all coincidentally without realizing it), and now we moved into our new home, May 29, 1969!

And that is how two cliff dwellers came to own a house they still call home now forty-three years later.

CHAPTER 5

A MAN OF IMPORTANCE

"Who," you may ask, "*is* Rene Anselmo?" the man from whom I borrowed $15,000 to purchase our home. Let me give you a brief idea who he was and how he influenced my life, as taken from an excerpt of "the Congressional Record" of September 29, 1995, in a speech made in the House of Representatives by Rep. Bill Richardson (from New Mexico) as he spoke his opening words in a eulogy to Rene Anselmo, just after he had passed away:

> *I want to ask my colleagues to join me in paying a special tribute to a remarkable individual whose long and distinguished career can be a symbol of determination, perseverance and audacity, Mr. Rene Anselmo, who died earlier this month, was not only the millionaire Chairman of Alpha Lyracom Space Communications operating under the name of PanAmerican Satellite, but also made a lasting contribution to the Hispanic Community by helping to create TVs Spanish International TV (SIN) now UNIVISION* . . . (Complete speech appears in the Congressional Record of September 29, 1995, P. E1895)

He was also named as one of the top ten of "100 People Who Made a Difference in Space" by *Space News International.*

Rene was born 1926 in Bedford, Massachusetts. His father was born in Italy but was raised in Chile and Argentina, eventually here in the United States, and became postmaster of Quincy, Massachusetts. When he was sixteen in 1942, Rene went into military service, fought in the South Pacific, and after leaving the military service, attended the University of Chicago. Upon graduating in 1951, he went to Mexico where he began producing and directing both theater and television and eventually made friends with Emilio Azcarraga Milmo whose father was the head of Mexico's largest media and television company, Televisa. By 1954, Anselmo was working for Televisa, marketing its programs to other countries in Latin America. In 1961, now president of Spanish International Network (SIN), he came to New York and built up the first network of Spanish language TV stations in the USA which showed programming predominantly from Televisa. By the early 1980s, SIN had become a major force in the industry.

When Rene eventually left SIN in 1984, he purchased PanAmSat Corporation, a satellite service provider headquartered in Greenwich, Connecticut and operated a fleet of communications satellites used by the entertainment industry, news agencies, internet service providers, government agencies, and telecommunication companies. PanAmSat effectively broke the monopoly on international satellite communications which was held by Intelsat, an international treaty-based organization founded and owned by several countries including the United States. PanAmSat, led by Rene, successfully lobbied the United States Congress to permit it to operate globally, competing against Intelsat. He was also incredibly witty with a whimsical sense of humor, and became famous for full page ads in the Wall Street Journal that depicted the Pan Am mascot, a dog he named "Spot," in humorous positions. Interestingly, he still remained friendly and would call me occasionally to let me know what he was doing, after I had left.

One day he called to let me know he was launching his first satellite and the details of how the purchase of PanAmSat came about. I told him not to worry as astrologically it was a good time. It was. It was a great success. Another time he phoned to tell me how well he was doing, and on other occasions, just to chat. I vividly recall a phone call from him when he was about to launch one of his satellites and I started to warn him not to do it that day as it was a bad time astrologically, but Fate stepped in. He received a very important call on his other line just a moment later and said he would have to call me back. I waited for his call for nearly an hour but I was working elsewhere at the time and finally had to leave for home and did not even know how to reach him. Unfortunately, that one satellite proved to be a disaster and it failed.

My last visit to see him was just a few days prior to his passing when I heard he was quite ill in Columbia Presbyterian Hospital in New York. I did not know the extent of his illness but when I saw him, my heart sank. He was obviously very very ill. I was not going to stay but he asked me not to leave and we had a very pleasant time together. I did most of the talking since he was extremely weak and I wanted to leave when I knew he was just too tired but he asked me not to, and I remained for over an hour and a half, knowing I would never see him alive again. I was truly saddened, and attended his memorial service a week later. He was one of the most interesting, totally brilliant unique individuals I have ever known, and despite our differences, we remained on friendly terms.

Here are a few stories of a more personal nature, not of his accomplishments but based on our association working together which began earlier in 1956 when he was just thirty years old, married with one child (eventually three children), struggling to get ahead, an American living in Mexico.

It would be impossible to condense what can be said about this unique "genius" with whom I worked and remained friendly even when I left until his death in 1995 . . . brilliant, totally unique, extremely witty, fascinating, marvelously entertaining, scintillating, at times enormously kindhearted, and at other times, when moved by his mood of the moment which set off suddenly—difficult, bitingly sarcastic, blunt, and completely maddening if one was the brunt of his caustic remarks.

I first met Rene in 1956 when I was working in a small office in Manhattan for a man who distributed films to other countries. When Rene would visit our office, he always took me to lunch at some impressively famous restaurant—his magnificent wit and great conversation always made it a delightful treat. In 1958, I was invited to spend my vacation with him and his wife, Mary, and five-year-old daughter, Pier, at their apartment on 27 Rio Poe in Mexico City. He was working for Mexican TV, at the time selling films to foreigners and would visit the man I was working for in New York at the time, a time when we were all young and could never dream of what the future held in store. With his totally unique inimitable brand of genius plus his earthy worldly acumen, he carved out a special niche in the world and in American history.

One day, I was invited to visit them in Mexico City, and at the time, he owned a very small Renault auto. For those who are not familiar with one, it was not much larger than a motorcycle with a cover on top. One day, he decided to visit friends who lived on the outskirts of Mexico City (Mexican "suburbia"), so off we went in this little Renault—his wife, Mary, six-year-old daughter, Pier, myself, Rene, and a box of two hundred baby chicks, *plus* the driver. I will never forget the sight of Rene standing up with his head sticking out of the car's open skylight while we were en route. How we all fit into this small boxlike container they called a "car," I can only answer "Quien sabe?" (Who knows?).

In the evening, they needed more firewood, so he asked me if I would like to go for a drive and see the small Mexican town; I agreed. He purchased what he came for, and we began our drive back when eight drunken natives started to roll the small Renault up and back with us in it, laughing and lunging at the car from side to side from both sides. I was very frightened, but Rene put his foot all the way down on the pedal, pressed it as hard as he could and off we raced at what "seemed" to be one hundred miles an hour, although I doubt if a car like that could do 50 . . . I am not sure how many were standing up after those wheels took off since neither of us looked back. It was not funny, but I now laugh whenever I recall the incident.

Later on, in 1962, after I had left my former employer and had just started working at NBC headquarters at Rockefeller Center, in New York City in their Operations Department, which was a fascinating place for me, I received a phone call from Rene in Mexico, asking me to come to work for him as he was going to open the first Spanish TV Network in the USA with an office on Park Avenue, and "we" would get rich. It was a dilemma, but because the salary was $25 more per week, which was sorely needed, it was a move that changed my destiny, although I look back with fond recollections of my short stay at NBC, and truthfully, with some regret.

Working for Rene, during the first year, I was left alone most of the time in the office at Park Avenue and 47th Street, as he traveled a great deal. In addition, I also had to make trips for him to other cities at times selling franchises for advertising products over Spanish TV stations. At one time, I met a Mr. Wrigley at Wrigley Chewing Gum, and it tickled my fancy to meet someone from the family who made all that gum I used to chew.

In the 1960s and 1970s, obtaining a TV station was very competitive and approval for getting one was decided by the FCC (Federal Communications Commission). This meant we had to present to the FCC a very compelling report based upon interviews with local politicos and other VIPs as to why our Spanish language station was needed in preference to others.

It was my job to contact, initiate, and make arrangements to visit these people and places spread throughout the country. I would set up interviews and then fly there to visit with the mayors, vice mayors, public advocates, district attorneys, community leaders, and Spanish community leaders as to why we should be given the license over other applicants. It was very interesting, and I enjoyed the people wherever I went.

We waited anxiously for FCC approval after everything was submitted each time we applied, and were very excited when *all* of our applications were accepted. I was also very proud of my own contribution playing such an important part in this—although slightly perturbed when I never heard a word of praise or thanks. When I would return, I was still doing all the other administrative duties as well, since the inception of the network I had been the only employee, until the addition of a sales manager and a secretary arrived more than a year later. I still performed the same duties in mentioned for a few years until we began to become successful.

The network grew with the addition of each station and expanded nationwide. Being a bit naïve, I had no clue how to ask for a raise, as well as a bit shy or frightened he would refuse and fire me. However, I assumed one day a raise would be forthcoming, since Rene was quite aware of all the super work I had done and the many late hours I was working. I was sure things would change when we became more successful, since we were not actually making money at the time. In fact, we were losing money to the extent that within two years, there was a question in Mexico about continuing the enterprise. Then a very strange episode took place unexpectedly (and shockingly) with a turn of events that decided many people's future.

One of the owners of the TV network in Mexico that was the source of our programming was a tall, impressive, and charming man named Emilio Azcarraga Vidaurreta, who was living in Mexico, and known to me as "Don Emilio." He was always kind and gracious to me when he visited New York, taking time to have a conversation with this somewhat shy young girl who was a bit in awe of him, always asking about what I was doing and about my mother's health, etc. I recall that each time he came he would ask me very politely if I would mind picking up theatre tickets for him and his wife only a few blocks away from our office, which I was always glad to do. Each time he did, he pressed a $50 or $100 bill into my hand! How did he know how I needed it! It is very difficult to describe Don Emilio in a few short paragraphs except to say that he was the brilliant genius of Mexican and Spanish language radio and TV programming who started out as a shoe salesman, but wound up as owner of one of many radio and TVstations in Mexico, and Latin America, building a complex containing 10 production studios which was called Televicentro where they produced programs for export to other countries with predominantly Spanish-speaking populations and finally entering the TV market here in the United States in 1960.

He entered the United States market by partially acquiring TV stations. KMEX in Los Angeles, and KWEX in San Antonio, which opened in 1961 as the first Spanish-language stations in the United States, and within a few years, absolutely dominated the Spanish language commercial market. In order to comply with the United States Communication Act, Section 310b, which limited foreign ownership of television stations to only twenty percent, Don Emilio Azcárraga also entered into partnerships with employees and associates who were United States citizens.

By 1983, over 22 years later, Spanish International Network could reach 90 percent of Latinos in the United States via its approximately 200 affiliates. SIN was then linked together by nine satellite-connected UHF stations, six low power translators, cable television systems, and five Mexican border stations. These border stations were actually located in Mexico and broadcast programming into Texas, New Mexico, and California. Legal challenges guided the Federal Communications Commission's decision not to renew broadcast licenses in 1986. A partnership between Hallmark Cards Corporation and First Capital Corporation ended up bidding on and purchasing the station group for $301.5 million U.S. dollars.

Turning back to its beginnings, after two years had passed since the stations in the United States has been started, Don Emilio's son-in-law, Fernando Diaz Barroso, also a distinguished younger man involved in the SIN venture, had decided to have a meeting to discuss divesting themselves of SIN since it was losing so much money until then. The meeting was set up for the following week in Acapulco. The elder Don Emilio Azcarraga could not attend, but Fernando would act on his behalf. Rene left the following week rather depressed and spoke to me about the possibility of returning to Mexico once again to live. He then flew down to Mexico City and would first pay a visit to his good friend, Emilio Azcarraga, Jr., (son of Don Emilio) who also had to attend the meeting. As it so happened, Fate willed otherwise. The two of them were caught in a massive traffic jam and missed the plane. They would have to catch another flight. However, the plane of the original flight crashed, and everyone in it was killed including Fernando Diaz Barroso. SIN, under the aegis of Rene Anselmo in the United States, then went on to fame and fortune, in an unprecedented success story.

One very special story that will always be remembered by me was when after hiring a few salesmen, Rene decided to open a small office in Chicago, planning to sell SIN time and for a possible TV outlet. He called me into his office one day and told me, "I want you to go to Chicago early tomorrow and stay there for as long as it takes, weeks, or even a month, to rent a very nice office inexpensively." A total perfectionist, "nice" meant "absolutely impossible"—low rents do not buy nice offices in Chicago. I was just married and not happy to leave my hubby alone for a long time and had no intention of staying there longer than necessary, but it was wiser not to mention it, so at six thirty the next morning, I took a plane to Chicago and decided to look around by myself, letting my instincts be my guide instead of taking time to visit realtors. I asked a cab driver if he would take me to the finest business section in Chicago. Off we went and arrived at a fashionable street facing Lake Michigan, I stepped out of the cab, paid my fare, and was on my way to make Anselmo's "impossible dream" come true.

"Our Wedding Picture"
May 29, 1963

I looked around at the mostly modern skyscrapers, until I saw an older graceful building with tall spires which I felt might be less expensive and asked the guards if I could speak to the manager of the building. The manager of the building was friendly and after I told him I was looking for a "very nice office with a view, but had little money to spend," he asked me where I came from and soon discovered we both came from the same part of Brooklyn known as Brownsville. There we were, two strangers reminiscing and sharing fond memories: he, now a building manager in a large skyscraper in Chicago, and I, working for some strange TV network for Spanish-speaking people known as SIN, when suddenly he said, "I have just the place to show you. Follow me."

We took the elevator to the penthouse that went into the spire of the building and stepped out into a strikingly designed very fashionable office with modern furniture and rugs so thick one could sleep on them more comfortably than on a mattress; but the best was "the view" where one's eyes could span the city as well as Lake Michigan. "How could we possibly afford this luxurious suite?" was all I could think of when I suddenly heard him say "and it will only cost $250 a month." He had to be joking, but it was true! It turned out that the man who rented this suite and signed the lease had owned a rug warehouse, and this was to be his showroom, paying a substantial down payment, but he unfortunately died shortly thereafter.

Sorry as I truthfully felt for the poor man, I could hardly believe what I heard. Within half an hour, with the signed lease in hand, I headed for the airport, back to New York, and straight to the office, arriving about 3:00 p.m. the same day (not a month later!) Ha ha! I tried hard to keep from smiling and to keep a straight face, but I almost laughed when Rene saw me. He was so elated when he heard the news, he called the newly hired salesman into his office and said proudly, "This is Freda; she has more brains and balls than all of you put together." And that was the first and only time I ever received a compliment (sort of, anyhow) and also the last time.

And that was the way of most working women who had to support themselves, support families, or even advance to a better standard of living while often working twice as hard and many hours longer, for much less wages and no benefits, as well as often being treated like third class citizens *before* the Equal Opportunity Act was introduced in 1962 by Pres. John Kennedy and reinforced by the passing of the Civil Rights Act of 1964 under Pres. Lyndon Johnson, which provisions forbade discrimination on the basis of sex as well as race in hiring, promoting, and firing—otherwise perhaps women would still be working under those conditions.

A year or so later, one of Jim's younger brothers, Tommy, surprisingly told us he would be coming to the USA; he had been offered a job by an American who had been in London where Tommy had been working at the time and offered him a well-paying job if he came to the USA as his construction superintendent, which Tommy accepted, and Jim was overjoyed that one of his brothers would be coming. Although the job was in Boston, it was only a four-hour drive from where we lived, so they would be able to get together often enough on weekends. Once again, strange things kept happening! A few months later, he phoned Jim, and to our great surprise, said that if Jim wanted to come to work with him in Boston, he would be able to get him into the Carpenters Union! We were overjoyed because that meant he could stay with his brother, work, and eventually join the Carpenters Union he had waited for so long and had almost given up hope would happen. He did come home every weekend too, and since I was once again working very many hours at my new position in TV, it would give us the opportunity to save some money, and we both looked forward to weekends when we could be together. It was rather romantic—two lovers who must part but meet each other every weekend. Besides, we had taken an apartment across the street from where my mother lived, so she would not feel alone, and I would be able to help her, leaving me little time to do much else. It was a "lucky break," or was it simply "the luck of the Irish?"

Some years afterward, a younger brother, Valentine, and his wife decided they too would like to come to America and would stay with us for the time being. Again, Jim was delighted at the thought of now having two brothers here. Val might have stayed in New Jersey except that the day after he arrived, we had one of the worst snow storms I could ever remember, and they shoveled for days to get rid of all the snow, so we could not blame him for eventually leaving for Florida to visit his other brother Tommy who had now moved to Fort Lauderdale. Florida, with its lovely swaying palm trees, beautiful beaches and year-round warm weather was much too enticing for Val to return to New Jersey. (Both Val and Tommy still live there today.) Eventually, both become quite successful living a very nice life there, and Jim would visit them when he could. Eventually, we became "snowbirds" (people who live elsewhere but come to Florida's warmth when the cold weather sets in for wintertime "up north"), and now the three brothers live near each other, often being visited by other siblings from Ireland or England.

CHAPTER 6

FAME "WRITTEN IN THE STARS?": REDEMPTION AND OTHER STRANGE THINGS

One of the mysteries of life are those unexpected moments that occur that change the course of people's lives or add some important factor that eventually moves it in a totally different direction than what might have been planned.

Let me begin with an unusual headline in a New Jersey newspaper *Trends* in the summer of 1966. We were living in New York City at the time. My sister, Dorothy, who lived in Lincoln Park, New Jersey, had worked as an assistant to the police chief of Lincoln Park in the years just prior to this newspaper article but had recently moved away. One of her duties had consisted of working with youngsters, where she was dedicated to aiding and guiding them when they seemed to be in trouble, and she earned an outstanding reputation for her work. It was not long before she became well-known for her ability in helping troubled children turn their lives around, many of them growing up to be successful, productive, and well-adjusted adults.

In the *Trends* article, she read about eleven-year-old Walter Salagal who had been missing from his home since June 4, 1966, and several weeks had gone by with no trace of his whereabouts. Disturbed about reports of this child's disappearance, my sister, Dorothy, contacted the parents and offered to help. She left no stone unturned, contacting newspapers, urging them to print the boy's picture so readers would be aware of his disappearance, and asked the FBI to intervene. She also contacted me because I was a student of astrology at the time, giving me his date, time, and place of birth. A friend and I worked out many different methods of astrological charts to see what we could figure out, and they all came out with nearly the same results. Sadly and tragically, it was our opinion according to the charts, the boy could not possibly be alive and had most likely met with a violent death, but his body would be found within three weeks of that date, around mid-July, near water. She then told a *Trends* reporter about our astrological findings. On July 15, Walter Salagal's body was found in a wooded section near a river in a place known as Two Bridges, in Lincoln Park, and the story about my "prediction" appeared in *Trends*.

This was not her only success in helping or finding others, too numerous to detail, but she also thought of numerous safety devices that have since been adopted in automobiles, as well as many other things that would be of use helping mankind. For instance, she wrote at the time, there was critical nursing shortage. "Why not start nurses' training in second-year high school as part of the curriculum? Many young girls with nursing potential can't afford the fees to go to nursing schools or can't spend three additional years after graduation studying to become nurses because they must find jobs. This vocational training would not only be an incentive to continue schooling but would bring these girls nearly up to par as registered nurses by the time they graduated from high school?" Truly, my sister was not only beautiful and brilliant, but she had one of the kindest hearts that can be found in humans.

After this article appeared, I was subsequently invited to become a guest on a very well-known *TV Show* hosted by Alan Burke, one of the most popular TV shows at the time, which led to another offer to write copy and do promotional work for a new "astrological perfume," resulting in trips to very interesting places all over the country, appearing as a guest on various TV shows. At one of these visits, I stayed at the beautiful and historically famous Hotel del Coronado in San Diego County, California, built in 1888, long considered one of the world's top resorts and also listed as a National Historic Landmark. This historic hotel has had many notable American guests including Presidents William Howard Taft, Franklin D. Roosevelt, Lyndon Johnson, Richard Nixon, Gerald Ford, Jimmy Carter, Ronald Reagan, Bill Clinton, and George H. W. Bush as well as other notables like Thomas Edison, Babe Ruth, Jack Dempsey, Willie Mays, Magic Johnson, Muhammad Ali, Charles Lindbergh, and Edward, Prince of Wales. Moviemakers found the setting ideal for films including *Some Like It Hot* with the famous blonde actress Marilyn

Monroe. It was a very glamorous and exciting place to be able to visit, and of course, Jim was able to be with me on most of these trips, so we both shared in the enjoyment of visits to these unusual places. They were like mini-vacations!

This was not to be the end of my unsolicited "moment of fame," when surprisingly and unexpectedly, my name and photo appeared over the next several years in issues of *Who's Who of American Women* as well as *Who's Who of International Women*. It listed my career, that time, as operations manager of WXTV in Paterson, New Jersey, together with my photo, perhaps because I was either the first (or one of the first) female television operations managers in the country at the time. I was amused and laughingly thought of myself as a "modern pioneer" until I received so much "junk mail" (unsolicited advertising), I ignored further requests for updates as I was never much of a publicity seeker.

Another unusual incident took place, in 1964 that brought back the past and changed my future as well as my sister's, in a much unexpected way when the mystery of my father was solved.

It all began by accident. In early 1963, shortly after my marriage to Jim, a detective was doing some investigative work with one of our TV stations in Los Angeles, California, at the same time I was visiting there, and on one of those odd hunches I would get occasionally, I asked him if someone could be found with only a knowledge of my father's birthday, probably using a fictitious name I had once heard of and who might be living in California! It was only sheer luck that somehow in the design of life, he managed to find someone who could possibly be the man I was looking for, who was living in San Francisco, approximately 345 miles away!

It was late Friday, and I was due to return to work on Monday morning in New York City; so very early the next morning, Saturday, I got into my rented car and drove to San Francisco strictly on a hunch, as no phone was listed. After locating the house and knocking on the door many times, I soon realized nobody was home. I waited for hours, went to eat twice, and returned again once more, waiting again for hours but it was in vain. Finally, on Sunday morning I had to return home without accomplishing my mission of finding this man I was sure would be my father, so decided to do some investigating of my own before I left. Not having a clue of how and what to do, I decided simply to ring a few neighbors' doorbells and asked if anyone knew the man who lived at that address, and if so, did they know how I might contact him since I was a long lost relative (it was not a lie, either!).

"Jim's Mother Sarah Flood In Her Kitchen, Wexford, Ireland"

    Finally, a nice young man told me that the man worked in Sacramento and often did not come home on weekends. My next question was, "Did this man possibly came from the East, New York to be exact?" as I was not 100 percent certain it was the man for whom I was searching. He was fairly sure he was from the East by his accent. I told him how sorry I was that I had missed him but had to return to New York, and if it was at all possible, could he tell me where he worked so I could call him from home? Honesty is the best policy, they say, at least, this time it was. He was quite sure he worked in some capacity for the governor in Sacramento (the capital of California), in some capacity in the field of safety issues, but did not know any more details. I thanked him and left for New York. It was not too difficult from that point on to find his phone number, simply by calling the offices of the state of California. Thus, after so many years, it seemed like the "impossible might be possible," and the day might come when I might finally meet my father.

Monday afternoon, I phoned and asked to speak to this man. When asked who was calling, I told a young lady that my name was Mrs. Flood, and I was calling from New York. She told me to wait a moment, and within a few minutes came back and replied that he was busy and if I left my phone number, he would try to return the call the same day. (There was no way of knowing who I was since I had been married just a few months and had a new name, and it was more than twenty-five years later.) He did not call back, and of course, I repeated my call again the following day with the same result and again on the following few days to no avail. However, as time went by, I gave some thought to the fact he did not answer my calls because he may have decided to check my name before calling me and found out who I was as he was privy to this type of information in his official capacity. Since his past life might be revealed, he would naturally be on guard.

However, I was not interested in revenge or with interfering with his life in any way but wanted mainly to discuss my mother's finances which I felt was his unfulfilled obligation to help; however, he had no idea of what was in my mind. Now I knew it had to be my father since logic told me no else would act in such a suspicious manner while working a public capacity. Undeterred, I kept phoning all week and decided that if he did not answer by the middle of the following week, I would fly out and visit him personally at his office (open to the public) and pursue the matter there. Perhaps he was a bit psychic as that very day he answered my call and with a gruff voice asked, "Who are you?" to which I replied as charmingly as I could, "This is your youngest daughter, Freda." His answer was, "I thought it might be you." And that was the beginning of a journey into the past and a future that was to change our lives in various ways. He knew now there was no way out with such a persistent daughter, a trait I probably inherited from him, since it was rather unique in my family, or perhaps, he may have felt his life and everything he had built up to then might come tumbling down, just like poor Humpty Dumpty!

However, I was pleasantly polite and expressed a desire to meet him after so many years and told him how very much my sister was looking forward to meeting him, as she always remembered him very fondly and longed to see him again one day. I spoke to him in a way that was not antagonistic, explained that I would very much like to set up an appointment to meet with him, and asked when and how this could be possible. He replied that he had to visit Washington, DC, for a meeting of labor unions. If I would meet him then, he would return later with me to New Jersey to meet my sister (definitely not my mother inasmuch as he thought she had a permanent warrant for his arrest! I had no knowledge of anything of this sort and doubted it existed, but he would not take any chances that it did). Secretary of State Willard Wirtz, (at the time of Pres. John Kennedy) was friends with my father and offered him his apartment since he was going to be away that weekend. Thus, the "die was cast" as Caesar said when crossing the Rubicon—there could be no turning back!

When I arrived at the designated place on Saturday, it seemed as if a meeting had just ended, and so I sat in the lobby, waiting until the crowd disbanded. Shortly afterward, I noticed a man with a cigar dangling from the side of his mouth, looking at me. Although I could never compare with my mother's beauty, there was a strong resemblance to her, and he walked toward me. After exchanging greetings, his first words were, "Well, you seemed to have turned out pretty nice." I suppose that was meant to be a compliment and allowed him to fully take over the conversation which he did, for hours. He had much to say, was very communicative, and, truthfully, had earned the right to be proud of all his accomplishments. He talked, while I mostly listened—a fair exchange—I learned a great deal about him. I left my questions for later, and he did not ask any, either! The following day, we headed back to New York by Greyhound Bus, listening to more of his adventures and arriving at my sister's house in New Jersey a few hours later when a strange thing occurred.

My sister, always very kind and nurturing, had eighteen stray cats living with her at the time, which were abandoned by others and somehow found their way to her doorstep and soon became pampered permanent residents. (Since then, I have always thought cats have a secret language with which they quietly signal other cats to let them know where they can find a great hotel, with really good food, and someone who loved them enough to pet them a lot!) In addition, she had adopted three dogs along the way, which were going to be euthanized, and she could not bear to let this happen! So, when she knew our father was coming to stay with her, she had a panic attack and was almost in tears fearing he would walk out the door upon seeing them and never return and was extremely nervous when he walked into her house.

When he arrived and walked in, he saw various shapes of cats and dogs sitting, strolling, squatting, and sleeping, and asked her, "Are these *all* your cats?" Her heart almost stopped beating, until she heard "I love cats! I have one named Greyhound and every night I take her out for a walk on her leash," etc. They were actually very similar in various other ways and understood each other much better than others might have (and more than I did). She was now in "seventh heaven" just at a time when her life had literally been in the proverbial "hell," and now when she most needed a father, he was finally there for her. To his credit, he did help; eventually help her a great deal. I was very happy it turned out this way and the longing my sister had all her life was finally fading into the background as he proved to a very important person in her life, and the love she felt for him never faded. That alone made me feel glad to have found him.

However, there was another important issue and the main purpose for looking for him. As newlyweds, Jim and I were living on a tight budget and try as I might, we did not have much to give my mother other than a minimal amount of money to help her, which was very painful for me. My purpose in searching for him for him was essentially to ask for some assistance for her. Since he had left when I was an infant, I had no memories of him, either good or bad. He was a stranger to me, and I did not want nor ask for anything else personally. Our friendship would have to be based on a fair settlement for my mother who was in very poor circumstances, thanks to him, and I strongly felt it was his obligation now that she needed it most, to help in some way.

I wanted to be fair to both of them and, after much thought, believed that asking my father to give her $50 monthly to augment the amount paid to her by Welfare would be very fair to both her and to him not much of a burden; he obviously was living quite comfortably, often mentioning the many stocks he owned (and to myself, I thought that the very expensive cigars he smoked cost a lot more than that per month!). How wrong I was!

Very bluntly and in no uncertain terms, he told me that she would get a small one-time gift of $5,000 for her entire lifetime of misery and not one penny more monthly! Taken aback, outwardly I remained calm, but inwardly I was extremely upset, since he had told me in his various conversations how he watched those stocks daily to make sure they were going up. In addition, he would be retiring with a very good pension in two years, and he lived quite frugally. I hesitated to say much then, wondering how to approach him in a way that would not offend him but suggest something that might be more amenable when his voice became "icy cold," and he stated that if I wanted to take any legal action, he would leave the country immediately and go to live in Mexico where he had many friends, but not a penny more would he give. I understood now what he really was like, despite other heroic actions that impressed others. What I heard made me feel very lucky I had never grown up with him.

Unfortunately, I had no choice but to extend to him some sort of olive branch because of my sister but for nothing else. He now enjoyed the loving family he had deserted and was now was part of it. While my sister was thrilled to have finally found her father and remained in touch with him by phone constantly, extremely proud of what he had done with his life and of all his accomplishments, I could never feel any love for him, although I showed as much respect as I could when we met only because of the help he had given my sister. When he retired two years later, he bought a lovely home in Florida where he rejoined his brothers and sisters with whom he had also lost touch over all these years, and would visit us periodically thereafter. Sometimes, my sister and I would travel there and stay with him, but she would not travel alone, and I was working very long hours so did not have much time to visit and, truthfully, did not have much inclination to do so.

My mother passed away in 1977, and to this day, the hurt I felt on what he did to her all his life and especially toward the end of it (despite the help he gave my sister which he never did before) did not completely change my feelings toward him and still remains a very painful memory I try to forget but lingers on. In 1984, he became terminally ill, and both Jim and I flew to Florida and took him back to our home via Amtrak (as he was not allowed on a plane). We arranged for a comfortable roomette for him with a bed for the twenty-three-hour trip back to New Jersey. Jim spent the night bathing and feeding him, as well as cheering him up with anecdotes about his life in Ireland, which he loved. He adored Jim (like most people do), and I often thought that if Jim had been his son instead of two sickly scrawny daughters, he might never have deserted my mother.

However, we decided there was no point in telling him he was terminally ill, so he was always quite cheerful, thinking he would soon be better, enjoying frequents visits from his other daughter and her two sons who were both now practicing attorneys, and a beautiful one-year-old great-grandson. After a five-week stay at a local hospital, we had him moved to our home and, luckily, was not in much pain thanks to wonderful hospice caretakers who treated him with gentleness, cheerfulness and great care ... until one morning, a few months later, he simply did not wake up, surrounded by the family whom he had rejected most of his life. It was the end of a life of one human being who had a chance to atone for some of his past mistakes, and spend many happy days with the family he had deserted who were with him at the very end of his journey here on earth.

Now I must tell you about a very important part of my life, something I had accidentally found, that would change my life forever.

It all started years before, when I was about thirteen years old and picked up one of my mother's books written by someone named Evangeline Adams—a book that thrust me into another world and changed my perspective of life and people from that day forward. It read almost like a mystery but turned instead to be an adventure into a world one could not see that helped me answer heretofore very puzzling questions. This riveting autobiography was called the *Bowl of Heaven*. Fascination with this book unexpectedly resulted not only in understanding myself (and others) but to interesting and lasting friendships, successful choices of action, and in developing a philosophy that has helped fill in the missing parts of my life, changed my way of thinking, expanded my horizons, and gave me the understanding to solve many knotty problems not only for myself but in helping other people do the same. I now share an unusual and fascinating tale, but it is only for those who have a lot of curiosity about life with its many diamond—like facets, those who like to mentally explore the unknown and are willing to venture into it.

The author, Evangeline Adams, was born on February 8, 1868, into the same illustrious family as two United States presidents, John Adams and John Quincy Adams. Despite her conservative well-known New England family, she became a successful popular astrologer and author with many world-known clients listening to her advice, such as J. P. Morgan (to whom she taught astrology), one of the most powerful financiers of the twentieth century who said, "Millionaires don't believe in astrology—only billionaires do;" Charles Schwab, American steel magnate under whose leadership Bethlehem Steel became one of the largest steel makers in the world; Enrico Caruso, the world's most famous tenor whose recording of "Vesti la Giubba" was the first sound recording ever to sell a million copies, as well as people like you or I, who came from all corners of the world to visit her. Her popularity lasted until her death in 1933 and afterward through her writings. In a curious and sensational trial that took place in 1914 regarding a charge that her profession was fortune-telling, a strange thing took place.

She proceeded to systematically explain the principles of astrology and offered to do a chart of anyone the judge knew, without any prior knowledge of the person. The judge, a bit amused, gave her a birth date, time and place of an individual without telling her anything else. She described the person with uncanny accuracy—it turned out to be the judge's son. Very impressed with the accuracy of her reading, as well as other proof of her work, the judge remarked that "the defendant raises astrology to the dignity of an exact science" and dismissed all charges leveled against her.

Her "predictions" were uncanny. Young as I was, since I was always curious about why and how things worked, I was fascinated and learned that astrology was *not* what many people thought, based on so-called witchcraft, ghosts, psychic ability, or mysterious cult-like beliefs. Her uncanny predictions were actually based on very orderly combined principles of astronomy, math, and history which showed that our planet Earth and people on it are affected by the moon in certain ways, while other planets affect us in other ways. Young as I was, my curiosity set out to find how it worked, and my life changed as I discovered "another fascinating interest" which eventually led to a "double" life of two careers simultaneously, one in the world of TV, and the other as the first teacher of astrology in the Adult Education Division for the State of New Jersey, again another "first." Once again, I was to feel like a modern "pioneer," and a very happy one too. I did this for many years, until it became impossible to continue both my career in TV and this one simultaneously.

Habits do not change much and now I have become an artist, known as "Cassandra"—another career! I truly am enjoying life now and grow wiser with age—like some good wines that taste better when they have aged.

CHAPTER 7

FOOTLOOSE AND FANCY-FREE: PALACES, GOLFERS, AND MARIACHIS

My husband's sister Beth

Adventurous and fancy-free, we decided early in 1966 to spend a little time living and working in London. It was the time of the birth of British music, as the Beatles, an English rock band, became the most critically acclaimed act in the history of popular music. England now became an international frontrunner for stylistic clothing, as Twiggy, the world's first supermodel with her skinny waif-like figure and boyish haircut, became the idol for millions of teenage girls of the sixties. England "rocked," and it seemed a happy place to live at the time.

Jim, as an Irish citizen, would have no problem getting work there; I, as his wife, was also eligible to work . . . so I gave four weeks' notice to my employer and quit the job where I had been working for more than five years. Jim had already left to visit his family in Ireland first and then on to London. I spent the following weeks in a complete frenzy, whirling like a top. Once we were settled there, my mother who had often said how much she would love to visit England, would be coming to stay with us. Leaving one's life and everything familiar behind was much more complicated than just going on a vacation, and a great deal of things had to be taken care of which took weeks to do. Since we would need a car there, I booked a cruise on the ship I was sailing, the *SS United States*, and the car was shipped at the same time—so off I went when all my work was done!

The cruise, the first I had ever been on, had now begun, and I looked forward to five glorious days at sea. The *United States* was the only U.S. ocean liner, one of the great symbols left of an age that would soon pass of decades of transatlantic travel by luxury ships. It was one of those magnificent liners now gone, like the *Mauretania*, *Queen Elizabeth*, *Normandie*, *Ile de France*, etc., with the exception of the *Queen Mary*, now converted into a hotel, museum and tourist attraction in Long Beach, California, still a magnificent symbol of an era gone by.

Although my room was on the lowest level below deck (the least expensive area), it did not matter. It was going to be five glorious days. However, it turned into four glorious days, because I was so tired when I arrived on board before noon, planning to get up at 6:30 p.m. for dinner, followed by and evening of entertainment. But when I woke up and dressed for dinner, I stepped out of the cabin to find everyone coming from breakfast for it was the following morning! I had slept through the night. However, I eventually went to many events, saw a good movie, as well as a very entertaining live show with a good comedian. At dinner, I was joined by five other people at my table, all from other countries who were rather interesting. Thus, I spent four—five lovely days until one morning, as all good things go, it was announced we would soon be approaching Southampton in England. Everyone ran out onto the deck to watch our arrival, which would take place in less than an hour.

However, I am not a lover of being in a crowd and went into the lounge and sat down. Looking around, I saw only one elderly gentleman at the other end who smiled at me, and I smiled back politely—we were the only two who had not rushed out. Soon thereafter, a waiter came to me and said the gentleman would like to know if I would care for an "aperitif." Aside from the fact that I do not drink any alcoholic liquor, I was more interested in getting off than in getting into any conversation with a strange man, so I told the waiter to tell the gentleman I would be going on deck instead a few minutes later. As I was leaving, the waiter said, "Do you know the name of the man who invited you for a drink?" and, of course, when I said I didn't, he replied "that was John Paul Getty," one of the wealthiest men in the world. Who knows, perhaps he might have given me some advice and made me a wealthy woman for life, but it was not meant to be.

The ship docked, and I was delighted to see my handsome husband waving his arms, smiling, and waving his arms as I descended the plank. Thus began an interesting few months living in another land where life was quite different even though the language was similar.

At first, we lived in a rented room in a house with other renters, until we could find a regular apartment which seemed pleasant, with a large fireplace. I thought "how quaint and charming," until morning when I awoke nearly frozen because there was no fire in this charming fireplace, and Jim had to light one, while I waited in bed rolled up in blankets until I warmed up, a procedure that would be followed during each morning, with each of us taking alternate turns in jumping out to light the fire!

After getting up, I soon learned that the word "toilet" over a door meant just that, and a "bathroom" was where the place one could wash in a sink. I was not sure where one "took a bath," and learned that that we could also go to the "public baths" where one could bathe for pennies, and take a really nice bath in a large tub where one's legs could fit in all the way to the other side when lying down (longer than American bathtubs). When one wanted to bathe, one was assigned a tiny enclosed room, and an attendant would fill the bathtub with very warm water, hand in a towel and a small piece of soap. If one lingered a bit like I liked to do and the water began turning cold, I had to *shout* loudly and say, "Number 5, hot, please" (translated "Room #5 *hot water*"), and in a few minutes, the attendant would have hot water in the tub. After a rather nice bath, one could also go for a swim in the large swimming pool for the same three pennies. These baths were meant for people who lived in "flats" where hot water had to be heated in pots.

When I tried to wash my hair the next night, the "machine" in which I put in two shillings (about one U.S. quarter), enough hot water would come out to last just a few minutes or so, which I discovered when soap was still in my hair not yet washed out! (Actually, most immigrants in the generation of my grandparents arrived in similar conditions when they came to the United States and moved into "cold-water apartments" that had large stoves in the kitchen in which one could light a fire. If one wanted hot water, a pot was put on that stove and heated by that same fire and the warmest room in the long "railroad" flat (as the rooms were called because they were one in front of the other like on a train), with only the kitchen or the front and back room having windows. (Eventually, when New York City prospered, these same houses were renovated and made into expensive one—and two-room apartments, because most were located in the heart of Manhattan where businesses could be reached easily.)

To look for an apartment in London, one would look for signs that were always posted either in the "laundromats," "confectionery," or "tobacconist" shops that sold tobacco, candy, newspapers, etc. We soon found a nice, but very tiny, apartment on the second floor in a very narrow house. The people who owned this small house were lovely Polish refugees named Braun, who had escaped from Hitler. The flat had a small kitchen that one could just about turn around, but it did have a gas stove, and there was a small sitting room and a small bedroom. The "toilet" was "outside," with no rolls of paper, but with cut-up newspaper squares and a toilet with a long "pull chain" and handle to flush it, plus a water tank. However, if one wanted a bath, one would have to either bathe in the owner's kitchen downstairs or in the public baths, which, quite obviously, we preferred to do.

We both had jobs now, but whenever we had a chance, we took a trip to some new and different place. What surprised me most was that one could walk in a circular path and, in a very short distance, see the main sights of London (which most of us have heard of in books or popular songs) in less than an hour without stopping—places like Big Ben, Westminster Abbey, Buckingham Palace, Downing Street, and many more interesting and well-known places. Buckingham Palace was a huge surprise: it sat right in the middle of a typical London Street with many small shops and vendors! Somehow, I had never thought of royalty being on a typical neighborhood street, so once again, life proved surprising and unpredictable. As an American, the changing of the guard at Buckingham Palace was an unusual and impressive ceremony to see, but mostly appealing because of those colorful lovely uniforms with huge high furry hats, as well as some very attractive soldiers!

We would also visit the homes of royal families, which had been opened to the public and helped to pay the upkeep of these homes in good condition. One could even sleep in an old converted canopied bed in an old castle for the night if one wished, at the right price!

Personally, what I enjoyed very much in Great Britain was the lovely manners people had, after all the "rather hurried" and sometimes thoughtless attitude of many New Yorkers. In waiting for a bus there, people would politely go to the end of the line and take his or her proper place. (In New York City, one rushes right up front and pushes to get inside as soon as a bus arrives no matter how long anyone else had been waiting. Also, New York cab drivers ought to go to London for a month for training before getting their licenses. Not only do the British cab drivers know every nook and cranny of the entire London area, but are wonderfully mannered and pleasant, which one could not say about many cab drivers in New York City.

Many things happened soon thereafter. A few weeks after my arrival in London, I received a phone call from an old boss who found out I was there, who "begged" me to take a job heading his British office, which oversaw other offices in Europe. What a fantastic opportunity—I would have *loved* this job, and this one would pay me well, which he never did when I had worked for him in New York. However, just like my chance to study at the Metropolitan Opera, my mother posed a problem.

When Jim and I were first married, we made sure we moved across the street from my mother so she would not feel alone. In addition, she was now a grandmother of two adorable tots, my sister's boys, and was totally consumed with seeing them. However, my sister moved to New Jersey, more than an hour away by bus, and although my mother visited them or they came to see her, it became difficult for them to visit each other, especially for her to see them. As usual, I was very busy with my job at SIN, working long hours, plus being just married with a new husband, having to shop, clean, and cook, trying hard to be a very good wife and homemaker, a totally new experience for which I had no experience. True to my nature, when I undertook anything important, I worked very hard to make it successful.

Things went from bad to worse. When I left for England, my mother felt totally alone, and within two months and a few phone calls later, I realized she was on a slippery slope and would soon be in trouble if I did not go home. Thus, I had to turn down one of the most desirable jobs I was ever offered.

Another important part of our lives were the close friendships we made and still have with people in other places. Aside from the very loving and close relationships Jim's family have with each other, keeping in touch by phone a great deal of the time, Jim maintains close friendships with friends from the past and the present. With many of these, they have one important thing in common: they all *golf!*

For those of you who do not know many golfers, please let me describe this phenomenon of golf. It is a fascinating and unconquerable game of great skill with many challenges that either results in great joy or great unhappiness, depending on whether one played a good or bad shot, or won or lost that day. Melancholia affects their outlook if they do not win, and they obsess over reasons they did not do well, what they could have done better, etc. It sometimes sends them into a "practice frenzy," hitting balls every day for a week, getting ready for the next game, but sadly that does not always produce the desired outcome. Their moods vary depending on whether they win or they lose. When they are not planning a game or playing many hours a day, they are thinking of, talking about, or watching golf games. Their heroes are Bobby Jones, Jack Nicklaus, etc. When they are very sad, it is because their golf game that day was not good. Perhaps psychologists will one day be able to help them.

We also met other golfers from different countries with whom we became friends. One time when we were visiting Scotland, Jim decided to see St. Andrews, the "Mecca of golfers." The exact title is "The Royal and Ancient Golf Club of St. Andrews," one of the oldest and most prestigious golf clubs in the world (the oldest being the "Honourable Company of Edinburgh Golfers at Muirfield"). The organization was founded in 1754 as the Society of St. Andrews Golfers, a local golf club playing at St. Andrews links, based in St. Andrews, in Fife, Scotland, and is now regarded as the worldwide "home of golf." King William IV became its patron, and in 1897, the society codified the rules of golf and, gradually over the next thirty years, was invited to take control of the running of golf tournaments at other courses. Its rules have been adopted almost all over the entire world, except for the United States (where this responsibility rests with the U.S. Golf Association, working in collaboration with national amateur and professional golf organizations in more than 110 countries) as well as a few other countries.

As I do not play golf, I went into the clubhouse to wait for Jim while he toured the course (and which subsequently became the subject of one of my favorite paintings, after I became an artist upon retirement a few years later). While waiting for him, I sat at a huge round table, one of many, while I ordered something to eat and opened my book to read, which I always do when I must wait while traveling. Soon, three attractive, tall blonde people (one man and two ladies) arrived at my table and politely asked if I would mind if they sat at my table and they were very pleasant as we engaged in conversation. They came from Norway (although one was born in Sweden), and two of them spoke perfect English. Their names were Birgitta and Lisa.

My memory once again did tricks during that conversation, and I suddenly recalled something from the long lost past, on my first full time job which was as a proofreader and editor in a printing house. One of my managers was a man who had emigrated from Norway after World War II, and would tell me stories about the country during lunch hour and said that I reminded him of the girls in Norway. Although he was glad to be living in America, he greatly missed his former homeland and would tell me about life in that country and how beautiful the mountains, the seas, and valleys were. His name was Clarence Ingebretsen, truly one of nature's gentlemen and was always very kind to me. I was so impressed, I told him that one day I would visit his beautiful land and now, many years later, it seemed almost prophetic as we made friends as I remembered what I had told him. It was a very sad day when he died quite young.

We were enjoying ourselves a great deal when Jim arrived and enjoyed ourselves even more, as most people do when this happy Irishman arrived. Finally, after a pleasant and enjoyable time, we all had to leave, and I expressed the thought that we should keep in touch with each other, so if we ever went to Norway, we would visit them and they could visit us if they ever got to the USA. Birgitta, the Swedish gal, said, "All you Americans say that but never do," to which I smiled and said, "Not this American. Do you have an e-mail address?" She replied she would get one, and we all went our separate ways. Within a few days, I received an e-mail from "Galatea" (Greek for "*she who is milk-white*"), a name popularly thought to apply to the statue carved of ivory by Pygmalion. In Greek mythology, he was a king of Cyprus who fell in love with a statue of Aphrodite, the goddess, who took pity on him and brought the statue to life, and he married her. In other versions of the myth, Pygmalion was a sculptor who carved the statue himself because he was disgusted with the faults of ordinary women; however, there are other versions.

Shortly after we met, Birgitta came to visit us when we were in Florida for the winter and to go with Jim to American golf courses for the first time of many. Since then, we have visited them in Norway many times as well, and these trips also included places they graciously and generously took us to—Denmark, Sweden, and Finland. They have since visited us in both Florida and New Jersey where we have our main residence still in Lincoln Park forty-three years later. All of us have remained very good friends throughout these many years and have great fun each time we see each other. They have become like "family" to us. Birgitta's brother,

Conny, an unusual, interesting, and charming man, invited us to his summer home on an island in Sweden, where they all went golfing while I read my book in the lovely surroundings of his home. (I hope Clarence is looking down and seeing this, thinking "I'm glad she finally made it to Norway.")

There was one other trip that we will never forget, which occurred in March, 1988. One of Jim's younger sisters, Beth, (one of sixteen siblings) had been living and working in Australia for about eleven years but had come to visit her big brother, Jim, and his "bride" in America. I had met her only once, years before, when she was an adorable, red-haired young girl sitting on a bike, shyly watching me. This time, years later, she had grown up to look like the lovely singer and actress "Julie Andrews" (star of Hollywood, Broadway, and London). She's like her brother, Jim; most people would fall in love with them as they "light up the sky" with their wonderful laughter and sense of humor, and it's impossible for anyone to feel sad when they were around.

This time, we were enjoying her visit so much, we decided to treat her to quick weekend in Mexico City (from our condo in Florida, not a very long trip), which at that time, was a very charming and quaint but very enjoyable and colorful place to visit, and, more so, to hear the famous "mariachi" music played by the natives. I was familiar with Mexico, having been there on various occasions to Telesistema Mexicana, Mexico's TV network, which was the original supplier of shows for SIN (now known as Univision) for whom I worked. The following day, all three of us were on a plane to Mexico City.

We hired a guide with a driver and cab, and were taken to every fascinating sight one could see (there were many), returning late at night near where our hotel was located. What a marvelous day we had, and now, we were hungry. We found a small outdoor café with a few people sitting inside, but none sitting at any of the three tables outside. Preferring to sit outside, we sat down and ordered our dinner. We put our small bags of tourist trinkets and our purses on the floor next to our legs and covered them carefully with our jackets, while we ate, laughing and reminiscing about all the things we had seen and done. When it was time to leave, we had a real shock! Beth's purse with all her money, passport, credit cards, airline ticket, etc., was gone! (For some strange reason, my purse was not touched.) We could not understand how this could possibly have happened since nobody came near the tables all during the time we were there! The only thing we imagined was that someone had a large "hook" and had reeled it in from somewhere else. We were no longer enjoying ourselves.

Shocked, we immediately hailed a cab to take us to the nearest police station, which was only a few blocks away, but the cab driver charged US$80 for a three-minute ride! Luckily Jim kept his head and gave the equivalent of $5, which was much more than the regular charge. Things were going from bad to worse very quickly. It was now 1:00 a.m. the following morning; we arrived at the police station but the police had little interest and seemingly were busy with more important matters. We left and headed for our hotel, where Beth immediately phoned Australia to cancel her credit card and was extremely unhappy when she was presented with a $500 bill for the ten-minute call. After a few hours of shuteye, very, very early the next morning, we headed first for the Australian embassy which, believe it or not, was located in the TV station Televisa Mexicana. The person who said he was the consul for the Australian government was a Mexican national and could do nothing for Beth nor would issue her a temporary passport, stating that he had no proof of who she was!

We were also horrified when we were warned that any foreigner caught in the country without a visa or passport would be jailed. Even the thought of Beth in a Mexican jail was much too distressful for me, and it was one of the worst moments I could ever recall. We decided to go immediately to the American embassy in the hope they might help us, as both Jim and I were American citizens. It was very early in the morning, and we're advised she would have to wait on a very long line to get in but under no circumstances could we go in with her which did not make any sense to me. How would they see out passports to know we were U.S. citizens? I should have realized it was because they knew she would be rejected. So many people were trying to leave Mexico at the time for some reason of which we were not aware, so she sat and waited on a hard wooden bench and I went across the street and had breakfast at the hotel where Jim was waiting, and we were still waiting there for three hours more before she finally came out and told us they could not do anything for her. Now we were almost frantic.

Jim came up with a suggestion for us go right to the airport, since our plane was scheduled to leave in just a few hours; "perhaps," they might be able to help us. We had no other alternative at the time, so off we went to the airport and were told she had to speak to a Mexican authority of some sort who had an office there, and so she went. Our hearts were pounding like sledgehammers, while we waited and waited outside not knowing what was happening. There was no other alternative left to us at the moment and the plane would be leaving very shortly. We waited and prayed . . . there was nothing left for us to do. About five minutes before the plane's door closed, she came out with a piece of paper in her hand, a certificate allowing her to leave—her exit visa! We raced as fast as we could and were the last passengers on the plane before the doors closed behind us. None of us will ever forget our "dream vacation" that turned into a "nightmare," but our prayers were answered. When we arrived in the USA, we almost kissed the ground we walked on, and eventually, Beth was able to return to Australia.

CHAPTER 8

AN INTERESTING LIFE

Before I close these chapters of the "threads of my life" that wove a colorful tapestry and continue on my journey wherever it may take me, I would like to narrate three short stories, followed by a few "words of wisdom."

The stories are true, although to some they may seem like "fairy tales." However, there is an expression that "a cat has nine lives," and while I never knew one personally that demonstrably had more than one life, that does not mean it never happened, since my knowledge of life and the universe, like most humans, is very limited. Thus, I share with you the stories of three clients who came for astrological advice, which (if you have limited knowledge of how astrology really works) may make you skeptical, but I can attest to their accuracy. These are typical of thousands whose charts I have analyzed, but if you have ever wondered, or have scoffed, at people who go to astrologers, these examples may be of interest.

Client #1: The phone rang one day early in the morning. The call was from a woman I did not know, who owned a local construction business. She said I was recommended to her and asked me if I would do a chart for a friend as soon as possible, as it was an urgent matter. Sensing the urgency, I asked for his date, time, and place of birth (if he had no "time" of birth, his chart would have to be "rectified" (corrected) to establish time of birth by the dates of important incidents in his lifetime, a very time-consuming process. I did not ask any other question nor did she reveal anything else, obviously a very private matter not to be discussed by phone. After doing the various charts necessary for determining what was happening to him at the present time which seemed to be very complicated and troublesome, thus taking over 4 hours for me to be very sure of what might take place, by using various methodologies.

The next day, my bell rang and in walked an elegantly dressed, attractive, well-spoken, and well-mannered man in his early fifties. He was alone. After offering him my usual cup of tea, my first question was, "Are you in trouble with the law?" His answer was simple; he came right to the point and said, "Yes, can you tell me if I am I going to jail?" I had to reply "I am sorry, but the answer is yes." He then asked, "For how long?" and I told him for "about a year and a half." I spent the next hour learning how it came about that he ran into tax problems with the government, and he did not deny his culpability. The trial was set for the following week.

I then asked him if his wife was very ill (it appeared she might have passed on very recently but I *never* mention "death" in the course of consultations, even when I am quite sure, as in his case, since it is not only against my principles since *nobody* is always right, including astrologers). I do not pretend to be more than an astrologer with expertise in interpreting facts based on many years of serious study and experience, and like all humans, not infallible, which is a gift only for the "Divine." He told me she had just passed away. Finally, I felt so bad for him that when he asked how much he owed for my services, I could not ask for any remuneration, but he insisted on it. Based on my advice, he took the necessary steps to get his personal affairs in order. A few months later, a well-written letter from him arrived from a prison, one of the more lenient types of prisons for non-dangerous or habitual criminals, and he thanked me, telling me he had another year to go before he would be out, but he was doing well.

What made this unusual was that he had previously gone to a very well-known local "psychic." Psychics are categorically very different from astrologers in the methodology they use (an error many people make who do not understand the difference). From personal experience, I have known two people who were born with truly psychic ability and from time to time did "predict" something that did happen, but on rare occasions. Psychics base their decisions on the "supernatural" and on their own "intuitive" processes, not on facts. Astrologers must study exact planetary movements that have been gathered over many centuries before interpreting anything correctly, most of the time. He had visited this "psychic" a week prior to ours, asking her the same question, to which she answered, "No, you *definitely will not* go to prison," and then charged $250 for less than ten minutes of her time. "Caveat emptor," let the buyer beware.

Client #2: Someone we knew recommended me to a friend who lived in another country. She was a widow and her son was a highly respected and well-known physician there. She called me one day from far away, stating how very sad she was, instead of being very happy because he had been offered a prestigious and very remunerative position at a world-famed medical facility in New York City, but it meant she would be all alone and would not see him much. This "sadness" was doubly compounded, because her only other child, a daughter, married a foreigner and lived overseas, so she hardly saw them as well as her grandchildren. If her son left now, she would be totally alone. I told her that his chart showed he would definitely make major unalterable changes in his life very shortly but "stars impel, they do not compel."

One can make choices when opportunity arises, as shown in his chart now, but the choice would be only his to make, and I could not tell her what choices he would make, but they will be major changes. Apparently, perhaps out of concern with his mother's grief, at the last minute, he did not accept the job—but it was "fate" that decided otherwise. The same organization and people who offered him that position made him the head of a new medical foundation which was to be based in *his* country! The other big change that did came about was when he decided to divorce his wife as he had been very unhappy for years—a fact I did not know—but now is very happy with his new career (so is his mother) and with his new girlfriend with whom he seems to be very happy—major changes as predicted.

Client #3: A friend of ours worked at a bar in a motel nearby and asked me if I could do a chart for a gal he worked with who was very interested in knowing if she would get married. After setting up her chart, I was surprised to see that men must be very attracted to her and that she would always be well-liked or loved by men, curious why she needed to seek advice since she seemed to have very lucky relationships with the men in her life. When my doorbell rang, in walked an unsmiling, very plain, almost homely, heavy large blonde woman, and although she might have been a nice person, she definitely did not seem to fit the role of a very popular gal to whom men were attracted.

Truthfully, I was afraid that somehow I had made a mistake in interpreting the chart, so I cautiously asked her if the birth information I had was correct, to which she replied in the affirmative. This now required some tact and at that moment was glad that my major in college was psychology—I needed all the help I could muster to understand how her chart could be correct. What I learned in psychology classes was that a gal who was able to establish good relationships with men most often came from having a very loving and close relationship with a father who truly loved her and showed her a great deal of affection. Thus, her expectations regarding men were based on the way she had been treated since birth by her father. When I asked her if she had a very good relationship with her father, she immediately replied that he adored her—he always called her his "little princess" and was very affectionate with her all the time. So far so good; I felt more assured. My next question was, "I am surprised you are not married already with this lovely chart; have you ever been married?" To which she replied, "Yes, my husband and I were very happy; he was wonderful but he died young, and now, I am alone."

At that point, I was confidently able to say "you should have no problem in meeting someone soon who will love you again—it seems as if it will happen within the following year." Her face lit up, showing me a lovely smile that actually lit up her face and made her seem very charming—and off she went. From our friend who worked with her, I found out that within a few months, a man registered at the motel where they worked. He was a German industrialist who was looking for a place to build a business in New Jersey and came into the bar for some good German beer. When he saw her, he lingered a long time, and he now travels happily around the world with his beautiful blonde bride! And so ends some "tales of astrology."

In retrospect, looking back on my many adventures and travels, the most important journey I ever took was on "the path to wisdom." From personal observation, wisdom comes not just by visiting other countries but by learning from others near or far away, by keeping one's mind open to new ideas but not losing sight of important values and virtues, by finding out how so many handicapped individuals are able to smile and accomplish wonderful things in life while other healthy younger people complain all the time about how hard life is, and also by avoiding "intellectual snobbery" where one thinks higher education anoints one with superior intelligence. Very often just the opposite is true, as attested to by so many successful, talented, renowned personalities and by those who live long, productive, interesting, and fulfilling lives even though they may not have had a chance to obtain higher education or were just not good formal students who liked to study when young. Rich or poor, formally educated or not, we can achieve many of our goals if we persevere, learn from others how we can achieve our goals and keep hopeful.

I would like to offer just a few "words of wisdom" based on my personal experience as well as observation throughout my lifetime. Those words are *"never give up hope"* and *"never stop trying to learn"* at any age. Keep trying, once, twice, three, four, or more times, if necessary, to think of solutions to problems, even seemingly insurmountable ones. Never be afraid to seek advice from trustworthy, knowledgeable friends who care about you. Do not forget to make new friends who have experienced life in many different ways. Good friendships are among a person's most valuable assets, even much important at times than jewelry and stocks one may possess and should be cherished as life goes by. They can be the source of much happiness as well as knowledge.

Believe in the power of prayer. Believe in the "impossible dream" but lay a good foundation, persevere, and expect to work hard to achieve this dream. "Miracles" do happen, sometimes when you least expect it. I personally know because just one of these "miracles" (of many) took place in a most unexpected way, as follows:

In 1970, I convinced the director of adult education in a town in New Jersey to allow me to teach astrology in New Jersey's Adult Education Program, telling him it was something many people liked and one day would be a very popular and important subject. This was at a time when astrology was ridiculed by a lot of people who understood nothing about it, its long history, and why it survived thousands of years and many generations, or why it was believed in by the most brilliant minds of each century since ancient times and still alive thousands of years later. Despite any suspicions and sense of ludicrousness of "why" I wanted to "teach astrology," it was strictly altruistic, hoping it would help others just as it did me. Since there were very few places it could be learned in those days, I wanted to pass on whatever knowledge I had learned so people could help themselves or give guidance to others. Astrology was a "light that glowed in the dark" when I had been troubled, and the knowledge I gained was my "reward" as it helped me find my way.

The director was a bit disbelieving, to put it mildly, so I offered to do the chart of anyone he chose, without giving me any information except the time, place, and date of birth. In return, I would tell him a lot about that person's abilities, temperament, etc. Within two days, he called and scheduled my course for the approaching season. That is how I became the first teacher of astrology in the state of New Jersey's educational system (perhaps in the country, as far as I could determine).

My method of teaching was by personal involvement. Volunteers would put a chart on the blackboard, and students would learn by discussing the person's life, career, potentialities, temperament, problems, etc. Students were from all backgrounds and walks of life. Some were highly educated, others did not finish school. Some were very wealthy; others were struggling to make ends meet. Some were unhappily married;

others hoped to find love and marriage. Some were on successful career paths, while others were retired or stay-at-home mothers—but all had the courage to try something unique. It was a wonderful class, enjoyed by all including me. I taught for many years and was also requested by other school directors to teach at their schools; time permitting, I did. My repayment was the students' great enthusiasm and enjoyment.

And one day, something very strange happened. If I had never taken the initiative to teach astrology, this totally amazing "miracle" could never have happened, and a life would have been lost.

One day in 1976, I received a call while at work in Manhattan to immediately come to a hospital in Brooklyn, where my mother had been taken by ambulance. It turned out, totally unbeknown to my sister and me, that my mother had been taken there, and the doctors discovered that both of her legs had turned gangrenous. She had never mentioned her condition to us, perhaps because she did not want to feel helpless, as she was always very independent in spirit.

The doctor advised me that there was only one solution—they must amputate both legs immediately, or she would soon face a very painful death. Shocked beyond belief, I knew my mother would never want to live this way, as well as permanently living the rest of her life in an institution, since I had to work all day and there would be nobody who could take care of her. It was totally out of the question for my sister to do so for many serious reasons, including her own poor health.

My mother had been heavily sedated and not aware of developments, but my mind was racing very swiftly. I told the doctor I would like to discuss it with her when she woke up and did not want to make any decision on my own. He left to return later. I immediately woke her up and dressed her, a difficult task in her condition, put her into a wheelchair, and wheeled her into an elevator close to the nearest exit where my car was parked—working as fast as possible, since I was afraid the hospital would prevent me from taking her out, but I was determined to find another solution.

Once I had her comfortably lying on the backseat, I drove to a well-known hospital in Manhattan where a friend of mine worked as a lab technician, and she immediately had my mother wheeled in, while I waited for another doctor's decision. Sadly, it was the same—both legs needed to come off very soon, or he could offer no hope. Somewhere, somehow in this world there had to be a better answer to my prayers despite what doctors told me. I was determined I would never give up unless there was absolutely nothing else that could be done. I had to try everything, possible or impossible (and keep praying!).

I phoned my sister and told her I was bringing my mother home until we could figure out the next step. My poor sister, who had very serious problems of her own, was totally distraught and saddened. For more than an hour and a half, all the way home to New Jersey over a bridge and through a tunnel, I was deep in thought, searching my memory for some answer about the next step I might take. Suddenly, something popped up from the deep recesses of my mind. I remembered that Gina, a lovely young student in my astrology class, had said she worked for a "podiatrist" (a physician who specialized in problems of the feet). As soon as I was home and had put my mother to bed, I phoned Gina. This kind, young woman immediately called the doctor for whom she worked, and he said he would come over when he finished seeing his last patient, in about an hour.

Although we lived almost an hour away, he was knocking on our door at the promised time. He examined my mother's legs, and as long as I live, I shall never forget his words as he said, "Most doctors will tell you that legs have to be amputated when they have become as gangrenous, but it just requires a great deal of patience and a lot of hard work, which most doctors do not do. But I have never lost a leg yet. I will save her legs." Immediately after the sudden rush of joy, however, there was something else to worry about—how would I ever pay him! Jim and I were making just enough money to pay bills, and my sister's husband had lost his business, so she had no money. From the moment the doctor said, "Do not worry—there will be no charge for my services," I truly believed that God heard and told his angels to help me!

Every other night, the doctor drove all the way to my house from his office in Hackensack and then back home for almost two months. There was a time he had to put my mother into a hospital for further care for about two weeks as she was recovering, and to his great credit, I must say my mother was not a very good patient and must have sorely tried his patience, but he was always good-humored with her—more than I probably was at times! Then one wonderful day, shortly thereafter, she got up and walked out on her own two feet with only the help of a small cane. Perhaps there is only way to really repay this kindness, and that is to tell others—"*never give up hope.*"

Almost always, you may find a solution if you pray for insight and keep trying different things and ideas that make some sense until you find an answer to your problem. Try methods that others have found to be successful or may suggest, even if they are not professionals, since professionals do not know everything either and make mistakes too. Search for answers to problems anywhere and everywhere you can—by computer, the library, asking others for ideas, and keeping in mind that life is full of surprises and sometimes wonderful ones. Do not expect the worst but keep hopeful and *keep trying*—you may find that life has more to offer you than you ever thought possible.

We Visit A Pretzel Factory In Pennsylvania
(Yr. 2011)

All paintings in this book are "Originals by Cassandra" as well as other paintings, and can be viewed at www.CassandraakaFredaFlood.com

Brussels, Belgium

Millennium 2000 Celebration